BOOKSELLING

IN AMERICA
AND THE WORLD

BOOKSELLING
IN AMERICA
AND THE WORLD

Some Observations & Recollections

*In Celebration of
the 75th Anniversary of the
American Booksellers Association*

Edited by

CHARLES B. ANDERSON

Quadrangle/The New York Times Book Co.

Acknowledgments

"Shakespeare and Company" reprinted by permission of Harcourt Brace Jovanovich, Inc. from SHAKESPEARE AND COMPANY, © 1956, 1959, by Sylvia Beach.

"Lo, the Poor Bookseller," by H.L. Mencken, originally published in the *American Mercury*, October 1930, is reprinted with the permission of the Mercantile-Safe Deposit and Trust Company (Baltimore, Maryland), Trustee U/W Henry L. Mencken.

"Censorship and the Gotham Book Mart, © 1975 by Frances Steloff, is printed with the kind permission of the author.

The Lindsay and Crouse lyrics are reprinted with the kind permission of Mrs. Howard Lindsay and Mrs. Russel Crouse.

"Vendor Librorum Floreat," © 1960 by Michael Flanders, is reprinted by permission of the author.

The excerpt from *The Customer is Always* © 1965 by Lewis Meyer, published by Doubleday & Co., is reprinted with the permission of the author.

Design by: Tere LoPrete

Library of Congress Cataloging in Publication Data
Main entry under title:

Bookselling in America and the world.

CONTENTS: Tebbel, J. A brief history of American bookselling.—Taubert, S. World bookselling: some historical comments.—Grannis, C. More than merchants: seventy-five years of the ABA. [etc.]
    1. Booksellers and bookselling—United States—Addresses, essays, lectures. 2. Booksellers and bookselling—Addresses, essays, lectures. 3. American Booksellers Association. I. Anderson, Charles B., ed. II. American Booksellers Association.
Z471.B63   658.8'09'0705730973   74-24294
ISBN 0-8129-0539-3

Second Printing, October 1975

Contents

A Greeting from Justice William O. Douglas   *vi*

Foreword   *vii*

I. A Brief History of American Bookselling, *John Tebbel*   *3*

II. World Bookselling: Some Historical Comments, *Sigfred Taubert*   *26*

III. More Than Merchants: Seventy-Five Years of the ABA, *Chandler B. Grannis*   *65*

IV. Best Sellers in the Bookstores 1900–1975, *Alice Payne Hackett*   *109*

V. The Future of Bookselling, *G. Roysce Smith*   *138*

VI. Shakespeare and Company, *Sylvia Beach*   *149*

VII. Bookselling in Boston, *Frederic G. Melcher*   *156*

VIII. Lo, The Poor Bookseller, *H.L. Mencken*   *163*

IX. Never Be a Bookseller, *David Garnett*   *171*

X. Early Years in the Book Business, *Adolph A. Kroch*   *176*

XI. Censorship and the Gotham Book Mart, *Frances Steloff*   *181*

XII. Bookselling, a Way to International Understanding, *Arnold Toynbee*   *184*

XIII. Lindsay and Crouse Salute the ABA   *187*

XIV. A Musical Tribute to the American Booksellers, *Michael Flanders and Donald Swann*   *190*

XV. Christopher Morley Speaks to the ABA   *191*

XVI. Mark Twain at ABA   *195*

Appendix   *199*

Supreme Court of the United States
Washington, D. C. 20543

CHAMBERS OF
JUSTICE WILLIAM O. DOUGLAS

September 23, 1974

Dear Mr. Anderson:

I rejoice with you and your associates
on the 75th Anniversary of the American
Booksellers Association, Inc. By reason
of our First Amendment, books are supposed
to be sacrosanct in this nation. Book-
burning is anathema to us. Prior restraint
is foreign to our Constitution, as are all
forms of censorship. At least in the
English speaking world, books have
acquired a protective position never
anticipated, I believe, when the bark of
the beech was the first parchment used.

Books, however, are easy and tempting
targets. Sedition--endangering national
security--is the ready instrument of
political leaders to suppress dissent, just
as heresy was the tool used by ecclesiastical
powers. Books seem dangerous to those in
power, as they traffic in ideas. And
there is nothing more dangerous than an
idea which reaches fertile minds.

Yours faithfully,

Charles B. Anderson
American Booksellers Association, Inc.
800 Second Avenue
New York, NY 10017

Foreword

Our book is first of all a festschrift, a souvenir volume celebrating the diamond jubilee of the American Booksellers Association. It is a historical record in prose, verse, and pictures not only of what has happened in ABA during the past 75 years but also of how books have been sold through the years in America and the world. It is a reference book, and on many of its pages there are lessons to be learned by booksellers today as the stories of the past are told.

The book consists in the main of four original articles. For the history of bookselling in America, a story that has never been told before, we turned to John Tebbel, who, with the publication of the first two volumes of a projected three volume work entitled *A History of Book Publishing in the United States,* is the acknowledged authority on the American book trade. Mr. Tebbel, recently retired as professor in the School of Journalism at New York University and a former managing editor of the *American Mercury,* is qualified for his assignment in our book not only because of his enormous research on the history of the entire book trade but because of his deep conviction that bookselling and booksellers have always been and still are important. When he was chairman, some years ago, of a postgraduate department at N. Y. U. known as the Graduate Institute of Book Publishing, he arranged that two of the weekly seminars be concerned with bookselling and conducted by booksellers. Mr. Tebbel describes his contribution to our book as a "brief" history. If time hangs heavy for him after he has finished his monumental work on publishing, we hope he may be tempted to tell the full story of American bookselling, unabridged.

The account of world bookselling is told by Sigfred Taubert, director-general of the International Book Fair in Frankfurt. Mr. Taubert is the editor of *The Book Trade of the World*, in three volumes, and the author of *Bibliopola*, the most impressive (and expensive) book about the retail book trade ever published. Through his contacts at the Book Fair and his travels throughout the world on Fair business, he surely is acquainted with more booksellers and publishers than anyone else in the trade. From the time he was a young man, he has made a hobby of collecting relics of the book trade, as well as books and articles about it in many languages, and his collection of pictures and books is probably the finest and most extensive of its kind. Mr. Taubert's article, submitted in German, has been translated for us by his friend Kyrill Schabert, formerly president of Pantheon Books, now a publisher's consultant in New York and an occasional translator of German and French.

Our third principal article—and not less important to us because we choose to place it third—is the history of our own ABA. We asked Chandler B. Grannis, formerly editor-in-chief of *Publishers Weekly*, to be our historian. He comes well-equipped for the assignment, having written the history of our first 50 years as a feature story for *Publishers Weekly* in 1950. What he has written here is an entirely new and far more detailed account of our first half-century, based on many days and weeks of research among the files of *Publishers Weekly* and of the ABA. His story of the last 25 years is the result not only of research but also of his own recollection of the events and people of the period. Mr. Tebbel's history of American bookselling does not go beyond World War I; Mr. Grannis in his ABA story, however, has attempted to round out the record by incorporating some facts about bookselling history beyond the ABA's direct involvement.

Another of our principal contributors is Alice Payne Hackett, who has written about the books that have been the biggest sellers in the stores for the past 75 years. Nobody is better qualified to write about best sellers than Miss Hackett, for she has been the official keeper of the best seller records at *Publishers Weekly* for more years than she probably likes to remember and has written several books on the subject. Many Europeans, including our friend Mr. Taubert, decry what they regard as an overemphasis on best sellers in America. In spite of the fact that

not everyone believes the emphasis on best sellers is beneficial
to the trade, we use such an article because it is part of the
American bookselling experience and because of what it says
about America's popular culture.

The rest of our book is an omnium-gatherum of short articles
and comments by and about booksellers, photographs of noteworthy events and people, and in the appendix, for the record,
a complete list of ABA officers and directors for the past 75
years. Though most of the shorter articles by distinguished
booksellers of the past have a vintage flavor, they speak a bookseller language that is as current now as it was fifty and more
years ago. When, for example, Sylvia Beach, Frederic Melcher,
David Garnett, and Adolph Kroch tell of how they got started,
they relate to us today. Every bookseller knows the agony and
the exhilaration of setting up a shop.

In getting the book ready for publication, I owe much to
many. First of all, I thank the directors of ABA for their enthusiastic approval of this project when I submitted my first
outline of the book four years ago, and also for their continued
interest. Next, I want to record my gratitude here to my friend
Joseph A. Duffy, until his death in 1972 executive director of
ABA, who believed from the start that what I proposed to do was
worth doing. I am equally indebted to G. Roysce Smith, who
succeeded Joe Duffy as ABA's executive director. Roysce's
editorial comments are always valuable. I am grateful, too, to
Sanford Cobb, former president of the Association of American
Publishers, who reviewed several articles in the book and offered valuable suggestions. Much of the book has been edited by
Mary Ann Tennenhouse, newly appointed to the office staff at
ABA as publications editor. With Mary Ann available for
editorial assistance, my task has been easier. I cannot say too
much in praise of the Frederic G. Melcher Library and of its
librarian, Jean Peters, who is a compendium of information
about what is contained in the books, magazines and pamphlets
of the book trade. I am grateful to my friend Bernie Mazel,
president of Brunner/Mazel Publishers, for useful suggestions
and for unflagging moral encouragement; and to Herbert Na-
gourney, president of Quadrangle/New York Times, our publishers, for believing that our book should be of interest to
readers outside the trade. Finally, I thank all of our contributors

and all the well-wishers not mentioned here to whom I have turned for help of one kind or another. It has been a unique and heartening experience to find that nobody has said no to any request I have made.

Charles Burroughs Anderson

If people get to believe that you know about books, you will sell books all right.

MADGE JENISON in *Sunwise Turn* (1923)

BOOKSELLING
IN AMERICA
AND THE WORLD

Thank God I am a bookseller, trafficking in the dreams and beauties and curiosities of Humanity.

CHRISTOPHER MORLEY IN *The Haunted Bookshop*

I hold with Charles Lamb, a wise bookseller does more for the community than all the lecturers, journalists and schoolmasters put together.

JOHN COOPER POWYS

The greatest public benefactor is the man distributing good books.

GLADSTONE

I

A Brief History
of American Bookselling

by John Tebbel

Author of *A History of Book Publishing in the United
States*

To romanticize bookselling by calling it "the gentle profession"
may offend the sense of reality among some latterday retailers
who see it as a hardnosed trade beset by difficulties which seem
largely incapable of solution. Yet historically, and even today,
the transaction between the bookseller and the bookbuyer remains essentially unchanged as the free passage of ideas from
the maker of them to the reader. As the middleman in this
exchange, the bookseller is not only the conduit between author
and audience, but in the conduct of his business he is in a
position to influence that relationship profoundly, whether for
good or ill.

The bookseller has always played this role, and others as well.
In the early days of the profession, or trade, he was often a
printer, a publisher, or both. In fact, the separation of printing,
publishing and bookselling did not begin to take place on any
significant scale until 1825, and even today there are booksellers
who publish and some who print.

Hezekiah Usher is generally recognized as the father of the
trade. He appears to have been selling books in Cambridge even
before he moved to Boston in 1642 and established himself as
an importer and exporter of various commodities, including
books. Two years later, he moved to another house on State
Street—"the street leading to the water," as his advertising
noted—and there, on the first floor, according to custom, began
to sell such popular items as Samuel Danforth's *Almanack for
1647,* which Mathew Day had printed locally at the Cambridge

Press, and later, John Eliot's Bible in the Indian tongue, along with products of the "great Mather copy factory." The succession of Mather clergy, mostly Cotton and Increase, produced 621 published works over a period of two centuries.

Usher established the pattern of bookselling-publishing when he began to issue his own books, such as the noteworthy *Spiritual Milk for Boston Babes in Either England,* by Harvard's accomplished librarian, John Cotton. The imprint attested a new relationship between bookseller and printer: "Cambridge: Printed by S. G. for Hezekiah Usher at Boston in New England, 1656." The phrase, "Printed by S. G. for . . ." marked the transfer to America of the stationers' function in London, where the booksellers initiated books, financed them, and sold them in their own shops at retail and to other dealers at wholesale. Some Boston booksellers did not publish, but in the early days, publishing and retail selling often went hand in hand.

Hezekiah was succeeded by his son John, who continued both to sell and to publish, notably the *General Laws and Liberties of the Massachusetts Colony,* in 1672. John Usher was a most unusual bookseller in one respect: he was rich. A contemporary wrote of him in 1686 that he was "very Rich, adventures much to sea; but has got his Estate by Bookselling." It was a misconception, however. John inherited most of his money from his merchant father, whose fortune was not built on his bookselling activities, and although the son was an even more successful bookseller than the father, his income, like that of his fellows in the trade, could not have been much more than moderate—a condition generally prevalent today.

These competitors of John Usher were a congenial fraternity, as booksellers have always been. They were men like Samuel Phillips, described by a momentarily transplanted British bookseller, John Dunton, as "the most Beautiful Man in the Town of Boston," who was "blest with a pretty, obliging Wife." Joseph Brunning (or Browning, as he sometimes called himself in America) came from Amsterdam to sell books on "the corner of Prison Lane next the Town House." Richard Wilkins sold books for years in Limerick, Ireland, before he fled religious persecution with two friends and established a new bookshop in Boston "opposite the West End of the Town House," where his charm and intelligence attracted the Boston intellectuals, who made his shop their headquarters, a development that widened and deepened in the trade.

Finally, among the early Bostonians who sold and often published books, was that complicated man, Benjamin Harris, known in the history of journalism as the proprietor of the first newspaper in the colonies, suppressed after a single issue. Harris, however, was primarily a bookseller. Arriving in Boston from London in 1686, he set himself up on the south corner of State and Washington Streets, brashly offering himself as competitor to seven other booksellers in the neighborhood, and attempted to re-create in Boston some of the life he had left behind him. In 1689, he expanded his bookshop by adding a counter from which he sold coffee, tea and chocolate, and with the addition of a few tables, established the London Coffee House, a resort so respectable that even ladies attended it to talk, sip the temperance drinks and possibly buy books. As a publisher, Harris immortalized himself by issuing the first American edition of the *New England Primer,* one of the truly remarkable volumes in publishing history. Sometimes called "The Little Bible of New England," it continued to sell for nearly two centuries and influenced the minds of generations of Americans.

While the printing of books developed with frustrating slowness in colonial Boston, because of tight government control, bookselling was less fettered and therefore relatively free to establish itself firmly. There were no fewer than thirty booksellers clustered about the Town House between 1645 and 1711, when a poor Scottish woman named Mary Morse accidentally ignited a blaze in the backyard of the old Cornhill tenement where she lived, and the resulting fire swept through Boston, destroying every bookstore in town save one, but it wasn't long before there were more booksellers than ever in business.

By the end of the seventeenth century, the bookshop was a fixture in colonial social, commercial and religious life. It was beginning to be a meeting place for intellectuals, and it not only offered a marketplace for native talent but also provided an American outlet for books from abroad. A single shop might stock more than a thousand volumes. It is not true, as is often said, that the American books sold in these stores were nearly all almanacs and religious tracts. In the lists of the publishers, printers and booksellers can be found reflections of nearly every public issue of the day.

As printing began to move away from the Eastern seaboard in the eighteenth century, and push over the Alleghenies toward the West, the press was an essential part of the westward movement. Sometimes it traveled dismantled on the backs of migrating settlers, or on horses and mules, and frequently it was part of the cargo of flatboats and canoes. Wherever there was a settlement, inevitably some restless printer turned up and began to unpack his type and handpress. In all these places, the colonial pattern was repeated and the early Massachusetts experience re-enacted. The first material to be produced, if it was not an answer to an immediate call for job printing, was likely to be a newspaper, then an almanac, and then a book of laws. After that, in time, came the reprints of British and native books, shipped in from the Eastern cities. Bookselling flourished in the front of the shop, along with everything from fiddle strings to patent medicines, and the printshop was in the rear. Often the printer was the postmaster, and his shop a meeting place for politics and intellectual and political discussion.

As in the previous century, there continued to be a lack of distinction among booksellers, printers and publishers, whether they were part of the westward migration or remained in the burgeoning Eastern cities. Booksellers continued to be printers in many cases, usually more often than not, and they persisted, too, as publishers. Some did bookbinding in the bargain.

The record is further complicated by the fact that so little is known about the early booksellers. The books that have survived them offer some information, since the title pages usually carried the name of the bookseller who had hired the printer, a practice common to both Europe and America, and begun here as early as Samuel Danforth's almanac of 1647. But this custom began to disappear after the Revolution, and by the end of the century, it had virtually ended, leaving place and date of publication on the title page, and only occasionally the name of the bookseller or publisher.

It was the bookseller, not the printer or author, who often undertook the risk of publication. As a publisher, the bookseller usually paid the author an outright sum for his book, or sometimes gave him a share of the profits. An author who insisted on keeping ownership of his property for himself had to make his own arrangements with the printer or bookseller as publisher, ordering a specified edition of a certain number of copies, and retaining the right of publication for a specific period of time. It was not until the second quarter of the nineteenth century that the royalty system was introduced, making the author in effect a partner of the publisher.

Bookselling was almost exclusively the province of New England until the eighteenth century. The first book dealer of consequence outside that region was Andrew Bradford, son of the redoubtable William, the first printer in Philadelphia. Andrew began his career in 1712 by becoming the government printer in Philadelphia—his first job. For the next decade, while he continued to be the only printer in the city, Bradford printed the laws of the colony and supported himself by doing bookbinding and turning his bookstore into the kind of varied merchandise mart we often see today. No modern stock of books, records, art objects and jewelry could have competed, however, with Andrew's remarkable assortment of whalebone, goose feathers, pickled sturgeon, chocolate and Spanish snuff, to go along with the books, pamphlets and almanacs which comprised his literary stock. Bookstores, in fact, were really the first drugstores, as we know them now.

Among the commodities sold by Yankee booksellers before the Revolution were Negro slaves. Only in the context of the times can one understand how a printer-publisher-bookseller like Thomas Fleet, an educated and otherwise compassionate man, could advertise from the Boston bookshop he opened on Pudding Lane (later Devonshire Street) in 1712, "a very valuable Negro woman about thirty years (sold only for her frequent pregnancy) with a fine healthy boy two years old." Fleet, primarily a publisher of children's books, including the probable first American edition of *Mother Goose's Melodies,* saw nothing reprehensible in selling a two-year-old child and his mother, and indeed seemed to regard this advertisement as contributing to his reputation as a humorous fellow.

By the end of that century, the decline of the bookseller as publisher was clearly evident, although the major separation was still some distance in the future. By 1799, there were only seven booksellers in the Boston trade who were also publishers. The most noted of them was Benjamin Guild, whose famous Boston Bookstore at 59 Cornhill combined his activities as publisher, bookseller, stationery and circulating library proprietor.

Simply as booksellers, however, the trade did a substantial business during the eighteenth century. An analysis by Clarence Brigham of their catalogues between 1734 and 1800 shows that most of the larger stores had from 1,000 to 1,500 titles on these advertised lists. Largest of the pre-Revolutionary lists was that of John Mein, of Boston, whose 1766 catalogue carried 1,741 titles. No larger catalogue appeared until 1796, when Robert Campbell of Philadelphia issued one with 2,100 titles. It was quickly surpassed three years later by the 215-page volume containing nearly 2,700 titles issued by the shop of H. Caritat, in New York.

These early catalogues reveal again, as Brigham observes, that while religion continued to dominate publishing in the eighteenth century, thousands of people also read novels, especially those of Fielding, Smollett, Richardson and Sterne, since native fiction writing had not yet developed to any extent. But book sellers did not have to wait for American novelists to provide what would be considered mass-market reading for those seeking something other than theology and similar serious subjects. Besides the English masters, as the catalogues show, considerably less literary works were available.

Before he went off to be General Washington's artillery commander, Henry Knox's Boston bookstore catalogue listed along with the masters such titles as *Delicate Distress, Fatal Step, Henrietta, Married Victim,* and *Rosara, or, The Adventures of an Actress,* all of them in two to four volumes. Benjamin Guild's catalogue of 1789 listed more than 300 novels of a similar character, including *Favorites of Felicity, Married Libertine, Suspicious Lovers,* and others not far removed from today's more lurid paperbacks. The famous Caritat catalogue of 1799 had 990 titles in its section devoted to romances, novels and adventures.

From under the counter was sold the kind of erotica which remained there until the Supreme Court obscenity decisions of our own time. While it is impossible to be certain, the first erotic book to be published and sold in this country was probably John Cleland's *Memoirs of a Woman of Pleasure,* more familiarly known as *Fanny Hill.* It was first advertised in England in 1748, and by 1786 the indefatigable Isaiah Thomas, the most famous bookseller-publisher and newspaper proprietor of the 18th century, was ordering a copy from a London bookseller named Thomas

Evans. Thomas reprinted it and sold it in his shop, and it was widely pirated and sold by many other booksellers. (The library of the Institute for Sex Research, founded by Dr. Alfred C. Kinsey at Indiana University, has a set of sheets from the book, retrieved from Isaiah Thomas bindings done between 1786 and 1814, so it is reasonable to assume that Thomas reprinted from the original copy.)

In eighteenth-century bookstores, *Fanny Hill,* under various titles, had to compete first with an anonymous excursion into classic Greek erotica titled *Aristotle's Masterpiece,* printed in 1788 for the United Company of Flying Stationers, as the imprint cryptically states, and illustrated with crude woodcuts. As the century came to a close, the trade was selling Sterne's *Sentimental Journey* in editions both intact and expurgated, since it was regarded by much of the public as no more than high-level pornography.

Booksellers were quite careful about how they sold volumes like Cleland's, particularly if they were men of substance like Thomas, and it is highly doubtful that publishers of Mathew Carey's status either included them in their stock or sent them out with such traveling salesmen as Parson Weems.

Certainly *Fanny* was not in the stock of Noah Webster, the other great traveling salesman of that century. Thomas covered the Southern territory primarily, but Webster traveled through New England as far as Portsmouth, New Hampshire, and down through New York to Philadelphia (and later through the South) trying to interest booksellers in useful and inspirational works, particularly his own spelling book, grammar and reader. He represented a class of salesman somewhere between the chapman, or peddler, who would sell anything he thought profitable, and the traveling book agent, who was engaged in selling the output of a particular publisher or group of publishers.

Webster's prodigious efforts illustrate how important selling outside the bookstore could be in the early history of distribution. He rode about the country, at first on horseback and later by carriage, establishing and carrying out promotional and selling activities which were not much different, basically, from those employed by publishers today. The only reason more authors did not follow a similar course was that few had Webster's ingenious mind and driving determination—or so salable a product as his speller.

Perhaps the most important kind of bookselling outside the retail store was the book auction, or vendue. It was primarily a nineteenth-century phenomenon, although it began as early as May 28, 1713, when a Boston auctioneer, Ambrose Vincent, advertised the sale of "a good collection of Books" at "Public Vendue." That is the earliest recorded auction. Once established, this method of bookselling grew steadily. By the end of the eighteenth century, it was firmly established, but it did not come into its own until the first half of the following century, when it not only flourished but had a considerable effect on the publishing business.

These were the solid foundations on which bookselling in America was built. Inevitably, gregarious lot that they are, those in the pleasant profession of making books, whether they were sellers, printers or publishers, or combinations of the three, felt the need to organize for the discussion of mutual problems, of which they already had a plentiful supply as the nineteenth century began. There was yet no retail bookstore in the modern sense when they met in the spring of 1802 to form the American Company of Booksellers.

The leader in this enterprise, as he was in so many other aspects of the growing book publishing business, was Mathew Carey, who had come to Philadelphia in 1784 at nineteen, a refugee from his native Ireland, where he had spent much of his youth writing incendiary revolutionary pamphlets against the British, who were constantly at his heels. On one of his momentary quick exits from the country to avoid them, he had gone to Paris and there learned the printing trade from a master, Benjamin Franklin, in the aging ambassador's printshop in suburban Passy, where he still amused himself with his original trade.

Escaping once more, to America, after a term in a London jail, Carey quickly established himself as the first authentic publisher in the modern sense. He was also, for a time, the new nation's leading bookseller, and in the course of what could only be called a full life, he wrote books and pamphlets, distinguished himself as an economist, and edited both newspapers and magazines.

It was Carey who proposed in 1801 that the booksellers organize. The first meeting had to be postponed to 1802 because of a yellow fever epidemic, but when they met at last on June 4, at Bardin's Hotel in New York, the fifty booksellers helped Carey implement his plan for a trade fair, like the great German fairs. His motive was simple enough. Such fairs increased the circulation of books, consequently more books would be sold. The first convention of booksellers in America was, in fact, a fair. The youngest exhibitor was Carey's eight-and-a-half-year-old son Henry, "who attracted attention by his precociousness," as it was said, by having a booth of his own. The booksellers of that and future generations saw a great deal of Henry. He was the most prominent of the Carey descendants who carried on the family business, and he flourished in the trade until he died in 1879.

When the booksellers were not manning their booths, they met and passed resolutions, in the immemorial manner of conventions. These were worthy resolves to which few, as usual, paid much attention afterward. The bookseller-publishers agreed to do their utmost to improve the quality of the books they were publishing; that took nearly a half-century to become reality. They resolved to avoid as much as possible interfering with each other by reprinting books already printed in the United States, and discontinue importing books where "good and correct editions" were already available in this country. Nothing was said about pirating English and French books, which soon became the primary element in publishing.

The new Association agreed to hold semi-annual meetings in New York and Philadelphia, alternately, and urged booksellers in other cities to form their own associations. Then the Company concluded its convention by electing Hugh Gaine as president, a belated honor for this 75-year-old Irishman who had combined newspaper publishing with bookselling during the Revolution, switching sides twice in the course of his opportunistic career. But he had wound up a respected bookseller-publisher, as noted for one activity as the other.

The American Company of Booksellers was a splendid idea whose time had not yet come. In its brief four years of existence, the organization was able to do a few things to elevate the profession, notably encouraging native graphic arts by offering gold medals for the best book printing on American paper with American ink, the best specimen of binding in American leather, and the best samples of American ink. But ironically, Mathew

Carey's original conception of the fair as the principal feature of the convention turned out to be a serious problem for the founders, since it enabled publishers in small communities through their exhibits to introduce inferior products which put unwelcome pressure on the city bookseller-publishers. Although the harassed Easterners could not be expected to see it that way, this development had, at the same time, a far-reaching and stimulating effect on the distribution of books outside the Eastern cities.

With the demise of the American Company of Booksellers, local organizations sprang up to deal with local problems cooperatively, notably the New York Association of Booksellers. These retailers were intent on curbing the importation of books, especially textbooks, and substituting American editions for them. It was too early in the day for such a plan to succeed, and with its principal reason for existence removed, the Association had disappeared by 1812. Elsewhere, however, the new local associations envisioned by the Company were more successful, and many of them were still active when the American Booksellers Association itself was founded, a little less than a century later. They proliferated, moreover, into county and even state associations. These organizations were useful in maintaining the stability of the trade on a local and sometimes even a regional level, but they were helpless when it came to meeting the great national problems of book distribution, especially in the long, bitter struggle over net price.

This was the festering sore that divided booksellers and publishers from the beginning. The principle seemed simple enough: it was only elemental fairness that the bookseller should get the same price for a book that was announced by its publisher. That was an idea, however, that was not universally accepted, since it ignored the competitive instinct to make a dollar.

This instinct was not stirred fully until the 1840s, when the first major improvements in printing since the fifteenth century —first the flatbed press, then the rotary press—made the creation of a mass market possible. The new technology was exploited at once by the first paperback revolution, beginning in 1839 with the appearance of *Brother Jonathan,* followed six months later by *The New World.* These were essentially magazines printed in newspaper format and containing full-length reprints of pirated British novels. Beginning as supplements to newspapers, they soon dropped that pretense and were issued, with covers that were lurid for the day, as separate publications. Sold first at fifty cents, competition drove their prices lower and lower until this factor and the Post Office's belated insistence that they must pay book rates instead of the much lower newspaper rates ended their careers.

Meanwhile, however, they had forced the book publishers into the competition, since they had been selling for twenty-five cents or less what the publishers and booksellers were offering for seventy-five cents, a dollar or a dollar fifty (at the most). Thus the paperback industry was created and thriving before the Civil War, prepared to come into its full flowering during the second "revolution" in the 1870s.

Many of today's major book publishing houses were in existence before mid-nineteenth century, beginning with Mathew Carey and his successors; quickly followed in New York by John Wiley & Sons, Harper & Bros., Appleton and Co., A. S. Barnes & Co., Putnam & Sons, Dodd, Mead & Co., Chas. Scribner's Sons, D. Van Nostrand & Co., and E. P. Dutton & Co., in that order; and in Boston, Houghton Mifflin and Little, Brown, along with several other distinguished houses that did not survive.

Nearly all of these houses had their own bookstores, usually on the premises, and many of them were magnificent retailing emporia. Where once the bookseller had done a little publishing on the side, now the publisher did as much retailing as he could on his own account, not only for his publications but for those of other publishers. It was a pattern that survived into this century, evident today in such splendid establishments as Scribner's and Brentano's on Fifth Avenue, Harcourt, Brace Jovanovich's store on Third Avenue, McGraw-Hill's on the Avenue of the Americas, both in New York, of course, and the far-flung retailing empire of Doubleday & Co. not to mention the numerous retailing outlets of the religious publishers.

For the small retailer of the nineteenth century, this kind of competition was not important. His struggle was with the publishers over the net price issue and the big discounters who sprang up after the Civil War, including the book departments that now became a part of large drygoods stores. Until the War, especially between 1845 and 1857, booksellers in general were enjoying the greatest boom the trade had ever seen. Cheap books were in their first heyday, selling both in cloth and soft-bound, priced mostly for less than a dollar. Volume made up for the low prices. Simultaneous publishing in cloth and paper was common. Piracy flourished, but native writers were proliferating rapidly. Competitive price-cutting was temporarily in abeyance, and prices in general were stabilized, with the fifty-cent book in cloth and the twenty-five-cent paperback as standards. In simultaneous cloth and paper publication, the prices were more likely to be seventy-five and fifty cents. Imported cheap English reprints also helped to keep prices down.

But retailers were being faced with a new problem at mid-century. At first only a small cloud on the horizon, the selling of books by subscription was increasingly visible. By 1860, most of the publishing houses were selling by this method as well as through the retail stores. As the tide of settlement rolled west, the book salesman joined the circuit rider and the district schoolmaster in bringing culture to the new territories. In his saddlebags or his cart he carried sample prospectuses for new publications for which he sought advance orders "or subscriptions" as well as bound copies of Bibles, dictionaries, encyclopedias, textbooks, histories, the classics, children's books and handy guides to farming, law, medicine and cookery. All of these, naturally, were in the retailer's stock as well. Subscription selling was well established by the time war came, and the conflict itself, with its outpouring of books about the campaigns and the generals, laid the groundwork for a boom in subscription books which reached such startling proportions in the Seventies and Eighties that publishers believed—and proved to be correct —that it was possible to sell almost any kind of book by this method, and in substantial quantities.

Booksellers, of course, were not called upon by these subscription canvassers who swarmed over the country like locusts, but by 1885 they were entertaining more and more of the publishers' travelers. The Brotherhood of Commercial Travellers was organized in that year, with a membership of one hundred, and mottos proudly displayed at the first annual banquet reading, "Competition Is The Life of Trade"; "There Is No Such Word As Fail"; and "Let Us All Pull Together." Toasts were made to "hotels and their accommodations," and to "railroads and extra baggage." It was still a rather small and exclusive club. The largest houses had no more than four travelling representatives, and all of them had formidable territories to cover, as large as all the major cities in the United States from the East Coast to the Mississippi. One Harper salesman not only covered New England and part of the Middle West, but included the entire Pacific Coast in his territory, while another had the South, the remainder of the Middle West and several cities in Pennsylvania and New York State.

The publishers could not seem to break out of distribution patterns that were as old as Mathew Carey's day. There were still two seasons, spring and fall, and in October the books began to pour into the stores for the Christmas season, with all the attendant evils that are still with us today. By 1914, the travelers had 3,501 stores to call on, according to the American Book Trade Annual, which meant one outlet for every 28,000 people. Rural areas were, of course, hardly covered at all. Most of the books bought before the First World War were, in any case, not purchased in bookstores. Ninety percent of them were sold by other means, primarily book agents traveling from door to door aided often by advertising. By 1905, there was also a great deal of direct mail selling by the publishers, using rented lists and their own—a practice widely deplored and attacked by the booksellers, as one would expect.

Harper's "direct expenses" for September 1910 illustrate the divisions that had grown up. In that month, $12,000 was spent for the regular wholesale trade with bookstores, $15,000 for subscription books, and $9,000 for direct mail—and it must be remembered that this was a much more equal distribution than prevailed in most houses. Needless to say, the new pattern of distribution did nothing to improve the continuous state of antagonism, in varying degrees, between the publishers and the retail booksellers which had existed since before the Civil War.

This antagonism reached a peak in the closing decades of the century. *Publishers Weekly,* the voice of the retail trade and its fierce defender against the evils of trade sales and undercutting, had put its finger squarely on the source of the booksellers' troubles as early as 1872—a lack of unity, a failure to realize that every member of the trade had essentially the same interests. "The retail trade cannot live against the competition of manufacturers," it asserted editorially, "and either the competition or the retailers must cease to be. The latter is almost the case now; nine out of ten 'book stores' are already mere fancy-goods shops, where books form the least part of the stock . . ."

Underselling was not a post-Civil War phenomenon. It had existed in some form since the beginning of the century, nor was it purely an American affliction. The Italian trade was complaining, too. American retailers were virtually unanimous in believing that the remedy was to lower prices so that not more than 20 percent could be allowed by the publisher. They protested the selling of books at retail or discount prices by publishers or jobbers, particularly when the publishers were advertising that they would send a book postage free on receipt of the retail price. Buyers who ordered from publishers got books cheaper than the retailer, who had to pay express. Most bookstores kept only two or three hundred dollars worth of stock at a time, and put their capital into sidelines. They competed with one another, underselling to get rid of books, which the general merchandisers offered at nearly cost price to attract customers for other goods.

Yet the publishers persisted in bypassing the retailers. A leading publisher told *Publishers Weekly* in 1872: "I'm about discouraged with the retailers. The booksellers won't order books unless you make them order. They will buy only what they must buy, after you've made them feel a demand from the public. So I believe in getting at the public rather than the trade." That was the general feeling among publishers. There was also speculation that public libraries might supersede the bookstore, and that in the future books would be borrowed, not bought. Others believed the mails would replace retailers as the prime distributing agency.

The price-cutting controversy spilled over from trade books into specialized publishing. A leading educational house issued an expensive book which was taken in quantities by booksellers dealing with teachers. These retailers quoted the books to teachers at the publisher's net price, assuring them that since the discount was close, they could not get them for less at the publisher's. But several teachers, not believing it, went to the publisher and got the same 10 percent off as the booksellers. When the booksellers protested, the publisher explained that they gave no discount outside the trade on educational books, except to teachers and clergymen—a large percentage of whom could be expected to buy the book at a bookstore. The booksellers were forced to conclude that they would have to confine their stock to one copy of the book, and lose money at that when they sold it.

When the booksellers, organizing some kind of resistance, came to a general agreement that they would not sell to any customer at more than a 20 percent discount, every buyer promptly claimed the discount, while the "book butchers," as the discounters were called by the trade, went on selling at any price they pleased and apparently had no trouble getting stock and credit, notwithstanding that most reputable publishers had pledged themselves to have no dealings with them.

The booksellers, then, were cut off from the textbook market by the net price system and the dealings of publishers with school and selection committees through salaried agents. They lost the market for quick-selling books by the activities of the subscription agents. They were exposed to the competition of every drygoods dealer who wanted to add a book department; and they still had to contend with the persisting "trade sales," chief source of supply for the book butchers.

John Wanamaker was the leading figure in department store bookselling and price-cutting. The first issue of his own literary journal, *Book News*, declared bluntly: "There are no fixed prices for books. Those which the publishers put on them are generally too high to be strictly maintained by anybody. They are certainly too high for our general practice. We consequently make our own prices. There is no reason why books should not be sold as handily as other merchandise." It was Wanamaker's opinion that "bookselling is a decaying business, here and in Great Britain."

As the century drew toward a close, it seemed that the eminent Philadelphian's gloomy prediction might turn out to be true. In a country inhabited by sixty million people in 1890, most of whom could read and more than ever before were able to buy books, bookselling at the community level was drying up. In Salem, Massachusetts, which had once boasted several retail stores, some of which became publishing houses, every bookseller had vanished by 1889, and the only outlet remaining for books was a chain drygoods store. One of the former bookstores still carried a few books, but the remainder of its stock was largely devoted to wallpaper.

It was no consolation to know that the problem was an ancient one. Adolph Growell, writing in *Publishers Weekly* in 1892, cited precedents beginning in 1668, and concluded, "When the history of the book trade of the world is written, the historian will find himself obliged to devote the largest portion of his narrative of the first three centuries of its existence to a record of the struggle between the bookmaker and the bookseller to maintain their respective rights and to break up underselling."

This conflict had reached an international climax by 1896, when representatives of the trade met in Paris to consider their common problems and attempt to find solutions. Every important country was represented except the United States, which had ignored the invitation. In America, to use the common folk expression, there had to be blood on the floor before reform was possible, and in 1896 plenty of blood was visible. But it had been there since the first attempts to do something about it had begun in the 1870s. Enough, however, had now been spilled to launch the reform movement that created the American Booksellers Association, whose history is told elsewhere in this volume.

It was preceded in 1872 by the American Book Trade Association, whose first president was a publisher, A. D. F. Randolph. The Western Booksellers' Association was organized in 1874, and soon there were new regional and local booksellers' organizations in Baltimore, Philadelphia, Rochester, Buffalo, Columbus, Troy, Milwaukee, Nashville, New Orleans, Providence, and Washington, D.C.

The object of all these organizations was to agree upon trade discounts, notably a 20 percent maximum. Joshua B. Lippincott, the noted Philadelphia publisher and bookseller, was the only holdout among the major publishers; he finally agreed to go along.

As for the buying public, it appeared to misunderstand the intentions of the ABTA. People thought it was a trust to keep prices high. The newspapers took up this cry, and some began to talk about the "booksellers' ring." Under that kind of attack, the reform forces were soon on the defensive, while the book butchers continued their bloody work unchecked.

One of the most notorious butchers, in Boston, conducted a lottery business in books. His advertisements declared that he had more than a million new and fresh books, many of which sold regularly from $2 to $3, but because he had bought them for cash during bad times, he would now sell them for a dollar, giving every buyer an "elegant present" in the bargain. His impressive list of premiums included $30,000 in greenbacks, $25,000 in watches, $45,000 in books, and $150,000 in other articles. This kind of thing drove several important Boston booksellers and publishers into bankruptcy, including Lee & Shepard, and it did them no good when the butcher failed too.

Inevitably, there were defections from the 20 percent rule. Libraries were generally opposed to it; the large ones got almost any discount they wanted while the smaller ones could not. The first annual meeting of the ALA in September 1877 agreed that the 20 percent rule was "substantially abolished" as far as it was concerned. It was increasingly clear that the rule had been a failure and underselling was as bad as ever. By April 1877, the ABTA was nearly dead, and with it the 20 percent idea. The Association's counterpart among the publishers, the Board of Trade, had expired a month earlier. That was the end of the reform movement of the Seventies.

It was followed by years of continued and often acute hardship for the retailers, and some difficulties for the publishers, who still pursued their business as individualists with little regard for the welfare of the book business as a whole. Ruinous trade practices continued unabated. To compete with the growing department store business, a retailer might have to deduct as much as 20 percent more on the book he had bought from the publisher at 40 percent off. Meanwhile, the store could undercut him even then by offering a book at a ridiculously low price as a loss leader. The retailer's overhead expenses averaged 15 per cent of the list price of the books he bought, while this figure was only 7 percent for the department stores. Thus a department store could sell a dollar book bought wholesale at 40% discount for sixty-seven cents and still come out ahead, but at that price, the retailer would lose eight cents on every copy sold.

One of the most exasperating things the drygoods people did was to advertise sales of standard works or novels at ridiculously low prices simply to get people into the store. Burrows Bros., in Cleveland, was so frustrated by this practice of offering "loss leaders" that for a time it advertised drygoods at cut-rate prices. It was only a gesture; book retailers were not really in the drygoods business, but the drygoods merchandisers were most definitely in the book business.

Plainly, there was only one remedy for underselling, and that was to reduce the percentage of discount to the trade, and lower the published price to somewhere near the actual selling price, which would deprive the department stores, and *their* competitors, the "bazaars" run by the butchers, from the leeway that large discounts permitted them. Some publishers tried to take this course, allowing a discount of only 20 to 25 percent on selected titles.

While none of the organizing among booksellers or publishers in the closing decades of the century was particularly effective as far as the individual associations were concerned, they paved the way for the permanent organizations that were to come, and inspired other beneficial efforts in related parts of the publishing business. Some were mutual benefit societies, like the Booksellers' and Stationers' Provident Association, organized for insurance purposes. Others were more like the New York Booksellers' League, organized in 1894, the purpose of which was to meet and talk about their problems over food and drink.

But reform was in the air on both sides of the Atlantic near the end of the century. In London, the Council of the Booksellers' Society arranged in 1895 for a conference of booksellers and publishers to discuss abuses in the trade, which were substantially the same as in America. There was much discussion in America of the work of the London conference, and it culminated in 1900 in the organizing of the American Publishers' Association. That was the beginning of the movement that soon led to the creation of the ABA.

In 1890 the U. S. Congress had passed the historic Sherman Anti Trust legislation, making among other things, "constriction in restraint of trade," illegal. Attempting a massive assault on the pricing system, the APA put forward a six-point reform plan in 1901 which contained a fatal clause. The members had agreed that after May 1, 1901, net books would be sold only on condition that the retail price be maintained, as provided by the regular members of the Association. Then came the defective clause: As a means of enforcement, booksellers who failed to sell net books at net prices would be penalized by a refusal of publishers to sell to them, or to distributing houses supplying them. Department stores were not specifically mentioned, but they were to be treated on the same terms as booksellers.

From the beginning, the plan was in trouble. After the first month of net prices, R. H. Macy and Abraham & Straus in New York were openly price-cutting a popular novel, and soon breaks began to appear in other cities. When the ABA held its first convention in July 1901, it supported the publishers' reform movement wholeheartedly, and at the end of the plan's first year, only Macy's, among the department stores, and Lippincott, among the publishers, were the major holdouts. The jobbing houses remained loyal to net pricing.

Then, in 1902, in an action which proved to be historic in the book trade, Macy's brought suit on December 30 in New York Supreme Court to restrain the APA and the ABA from enforcing the rules against underselling. They also asked a perpetual injunction against the defendants' blacklisting of them, and from "resorting to any species of threat to compel them to join either of the associations or to maintain the prices of books." The complaint asked that a temporary injunction be granted pending the trial of the action, and that a referee be appointed to take proof of the damages sustained by the plaintiff, which were put at $100,000. A judgment was further demanded that the "agreements between the associations to maintain prices and prevent competition be declared unlawful and null and void."

Colonel Stephen H. Olin, counsel for the APA, filed a memorandum arguing that a copyright book is an article on which by provision of law, and indeed of the Constitution, the proprietor has a right to fix a price. Thus the groundwork was established for an historic controversy.

The court battle was fought chiefly on copyright books. Earlier decisions had indicated that the proprietor of a monopoly article protected by a United States patent or copyright law had an absolute right to control the prices indirectly through the distributing agency as well as in his own sales. But, it was argued, the department stores were not entitled to discounts on non-copyright books, because that would give them a margin of profit as a basis for cutting prices. In the area of copyright books, most of the department stores accepted the reform. Macy's objected.

The case dragged on through the courts, from appeal to appeal, until the Supreme Court of the United States handed down a unanimous opinion on December 1, 1913, that copyright as well as patent property is not exempt from the provisions of the

Sherman Anti-Trust Law against combination in restraint of trade. The decision was against the APA, and inferentially against any other combination of producers or dealers who desired to control a product or property other than their own.

Thus the Macy case ended after more than thirteen years, with damages assessed by the courts at $140,000. Miss E. L. Kinnear, book buyer for the store during the conflict, was now free to tell how she survived, and it was clear from her account that lack of unity was again the villain. Unable to buy books in the firm's name or in her own name from publishers, she had turned to relatives and friends and at one time had eighteen surrogates buying books and turning them over to her. She found booksellers as far South as Texas and as far West as Denver who were in sympathy. They bought books and shipped them to Macy's. Those who were discovered by the APA to be engaging in this practice were warned to stop, and of those who refused, some were driven out of business. Most declined, however, to ruin themselves for Macy's. The store even opened book shops in other cities to get books. These establishments were stocked, and then the books would be reshipped to New York. Miss Kinnear's house in Chelsea was watched day and night by detectives, some of whom tried to persuade the postman to show them her letters so that the cooperating stores could be traced.

When commission and freight charges were added, the ultimate price of books the store acquired was never far from the price at which Macy's sold them, but even so, they were never sold at less than they cost the store.

PW had a final comment on the Macy case: "Thirteen years ago price cutting was rampant; the trade was disorganized; conditions were verging on the chaotic, and the book business of the country was fast falling into suicidal destruction. The Macy cases may have brought knowledge that any attempt to maintain prices by coercion or concerted action of any sort whatsoever is illegal. But they have also brought knowledge that net prices maintained, not by coercion, but by individual choice, bring trade solidarity and make prosperity, if not probable, at least possible. And they have accomplished a further equally general realization that unwarranted 'cut prices' are a stupendous merchandizing blunder, if not actually immoral or illegal."

The end of the Macy case signaled the end of the APA. It dissolved late in 1914. To the end, its members and friends denied that it had any resemblance to a book trust, or that it had tried to stifle competition, but neither the general public nor the Supreme Court believed them. The publishers were now left without any form of organization except for the American Publishers' Copyright League, and so on the eve of the Great War, the booksellers were united through the ABA in what had become a growing organization of increasing effectiveness, while the publishers remained unorganized individualists for the most part, as they had been from the beginning. And as George Brett of the Macmillan Company observed in the *Atlantic Monthly* for April 1913, the chief problem in the book business was still inadequate distribution.

The rest is part of the history of ABA, told elsewhere in this book. It may be small comfort, but the history set down here demonstrates rather clearly that the problems of booksellers are perennial and of long standing. What is more comforting is that every time the trade has been left for dead by any of the shifting economic and cultural developments in American life, it has shown a capacity not only to survive but often to make a virtue out of adversity. The retail bookseller and the publisher learned to live with the department store bookstore, not as a result of the Macy decision but because the trade expanded enough to make economic cohabitation possible and many of them sold their books at publishers' list prices. Price-cutting could not be ended, but in another way it became useful to publishers as a means of disposing of remainders at something less than a total loss, and with a profit to the bookseller.

That is not to say there has been a plethora of silver linings in the history of twentieth century bookselling. Far from it. Some antagonism between publishers and booksellers may persist to a limited extent covering much the same ground as it has for the past hundred years. On the other hand strong top-level liaison committees between the AAP and the ABA, as well as between the AAP and the National Association of College Stores are meeting regularly to discuss basic problems of book promotion and distribution, and these discussions are bearing fruit. The book business remains a highly individualistic profession on both sides, and any kind of cooperation is difficult to achieve. The publishers are organized again, and the Association of

American Publishers has some dissenters and lukewarm members, just as the earlier APA had around the turn of the Century, though it is making a strong representation of the book trade's case in Washington. The booksellers are, amazingly, stronger than ever in spite of this century's Depression, a second Great War, and the wholly unforeseen advent of television as a competitor.

Television, in fact, is a testimony to the vitality of bookselling. It came as the climax to a long line of potential book-killers beginning in the 1890's with the explosion of the bicycle craze, when it appeared that most of America was destined to spend much of its time traveling around on two wheels. There were a good many early day McLuhans who pronounced reading as dead, and particularly the book, which took more time to consume than magazines.

But people somehow found time to read books when they were not bicycling, just as successively they managed to find it when they were not motoring, or watching movies, or listening to the radio. Books were declared obsolete, even by some booksellers, with the appearance of each of these phenomena.

It is true that radio changed the character of publishing somewhat, as none of the others had done, but not in the way it had been feared. The immense popularity of thrillers, dramas and other kinds of radio entertainment appeared only to increase the public appetite for detective novels and fiction generally, and led to increased production of plays between book covers. Television, when it came into full bloom in the Fifties, unquestionably hurt publishing for a time, as it did every other competing medium. But once the novelty wore off and a certain monotony set in, book reading and bookselling continued to increase, and again the reading audience was widened by what was seen on the tube. Contrary to the doomsayers, book production has increased every year and it is the television audience that now shows a decline. Television has, in fact, become a major publicity device through which to expose books and their authors to the public.

Book clubs were also believed to threaten booksellers when they first began to proliferate and attract large memberships, after having existed since 1825. But their advertising, and their penetration of the mass market, like mail-order selling and the subscription book business before them, only served to increase the reading public and in the end they have stimulated retail sales.

The problems remain. Profit margins are still small, as they have always been, and easily wiped out. While there are still some notably successful personal bookstores, mounting costs have encouraged the adoption of "self-service" and the advent of the suburban shopping center has encouraged the establishment of large new chains of stores which while they have broadened the market have in most cases had to limit their stock mainly to potentially fast moving items and remainders. Computerization in the industry initially may have created more headaches than it has cured, but the adoption of data processed inventory control may ultimately help to reduce costs. Then there are space, overhead, shipping, inflation, billing procedures—every bookseller has his own list of troubles.

The gentle profession, if it is still permissible to call it that, has always responded, however inadequately, to social pressures. For example, women have been important in bookselling for more than a hundred years, and today, as everyone knows, they play an indispensable role, while they have only recently begun to make a real place for themselves in publishing.

Economic pressures have always made bookselling a precarious profession but to many of those who stay in it when they would be richer and less harassed in some other occupation, it offers the same rewards Hezekiah Usher and his son John found in the first bookstore. In essence, bookselling is a marrying of minds, not only through the ideas and emotions that books convey to readers and sellers, but among all those literate people who make, sell and buy books. In an unhappy world, they may well be the happiest fraternity remaining to us.

II

World Bookselling:
Some Historical Comments

by Sigfred Taubert

Author of *Bibliopola**
Translated from the German by Kyrill Schabert

> In those days, ten ordinary histories of Kings and Courtiers were
> well exchanged against the tenth part of one good history of
> booksellers.
>
> —THOMAS CARLYLE

I confess that the invitation of the ABA to write a summary of
the history of world bookselling past and present for its anniversary publication was quite tempting. But fascinated as I was by
the idea, my enthusiasm was dampened by the realization that
there are basic problems with such a project. To this day most
countries have little recorded information about bookselling
and it is therefore difficult to compile a general history of the
field. Although I have wondered how wise it is to attempt the
task at all, after much soulsearching I agreed to do it, even
though fully aware that I would be frustrated by the scarcity of
available material. I hope this contribution will at least make all
bibliophiles aware of the extent to which this part of our cultural
and economic heritage remains largely unexplored.

There are many reasons for this unfortunate situation. First,
even countries with a literary tradition have failed to recognize
the importance of bookselling; indeed, we find modern historians treating the history of bookselling with a degree of con-

*The illustrations accompanying this article are taken from Mr. Taubert's two-volume
work *Bibliopola* and are used with the kind permission of the publisher. The captions for
these illustrations were translated by Charles B. Anderson.

tempt. And, bookselling was not a trade to excite succeeding generations unless it was allied with the more stimulating activities of publishing and printing. Thus, many important criteria went unrecorded, which in a sense holds true even today. Only to a limited degree can we reconstruct the functions of a publisher-bookseller by means of his output. The retail bookseller did not offer a base from which to proceed unless he left behind autobiographical material, which was rarely the case. But we can learn from the catalogues and records of reading rooms and lending libraries which fulfilled an important function in the 18th and 19th Centuries and which serve us as the base for an exploratory and scientific investigation in this field.

No wonder that the many histories of the book concentrate on publisher-booksellers while the retail bookseller as such has been relegated to a modest role. Existing monographs on specific aspects of the world of books are almost exclusively concerned with the publishing end of the book trade. The lack of attention given to retail bookselling in modern reference works on the history of books is woefully deficient. In a publication such as *The Bookman's Glossary* by M. C. Turner (New York 1961)

Figure 1. There is no such thing as a pictorial reproduction of a bookstore from classical Greece or Rome that has been accepted as authentic beyond any doubt. It is quite possible however, that this late Roman illustration from about 100 A.D. is a "Taberna Libraria," or in other words, a bookstore. Attached to the front of most of the handwritten scrolls on display are what may be described as labels indicating titles.

or *The Glossary of the Book* by G. A. Glaister (London 1960) one searches in vain for any reference to bookselling. Obviously its existence is considered not worth mentioning.

The International Publishers Association in its *Vocabulaire technique de l'éditeur en sept langues* published in 1913 attempted to examine the retail book trade in its diverse aspects. Their broad approach to the subject is interesting reading even today. In Volume 1 of the *Lexikon des gesamten Buchwesens* (Leipzig 1935) we find "booksellers" defined as all who are professionally engaged in the manufacture and distribution of books, especially as the term applies to the retail bookseller. Even today that definition is an acceptable one. A somewhat more emotional albeit less embracing definition of retail bookselling is to be found in the *Encyclopedia of Library and Information Science* (Vol. 111, New York 1970) under the heading "Bookstores."

"Since the era of Alexander the Great the bookstore has been more than a stocking place for books. Booksellers have been lovers of books—some more scrupulous than others, but still men who placed the love of books before their own gain and comfort." Unfortunately here again no attempt is made to pay tribute to the retail trade by defining its past and present role.

It is quite apparent, then, that we are on shaky ground. Modern man has come to regard the printed word as the most important medium of the diverse forms of communication. He tends to ignore the fact that prior to the invention and use of printing and in a broader sense prior to the written record of human thought and emotion the generations were linked by oral communication. This should be kept in mind because a weighted examination of the history of the book trade as it relates to the different parts of the world must take into account the existence of a tradition preserved by word of mouth. It would therefore be misleading to apply the presence of a relatively sophisticated book trade as the sole criterion in making comparisons on an international scale. Of course we find ourselves on safer ground in countries where history is closely linked to the written and printed word. But the moment we compare the literary tradition of Europe with that of Africa in an attempt to find a link between the past and the present of the book trade we are confronted by a different picture.

This point, which I can mention only briefly, is bound to cause a shift in the emphasis usually given to the printed word, its extraordinary significance, and with it the primary role of the book trade. It is hoped that any history of the book trade still to be written will consider these aspects. The stories, legends and fairy tales of a civilization based on an oral tradition surely are not to be regarded as historical phenomena of the book trade. Nevertheless their time and circumstances must be viewed in the context of the legacy of the book in its relationship to our historical development.

We shall try to trace the early evidences of book trading and highlight its development through the centuries. In doing so we will find, contrary to common belief, that a book trade existed before the advent of the printing press.

Asia

Let us therefore begin our exploration with Asia, then continue through Europe to the New World and conclude with Africa and Australia. This follows the course of evolution and the growth of the art of printing which developed independently in Asia and Europe. Nevertheless it was from Europe that book printing began its triumphant procession throughout the whole world.

The independent development of the art of printing, first in East Asia, and then in Europe, began in China. There is ample evidence that rubbings of religious texts on stone were known in the 6th century and that wood block printing, so suited to Chinese characters, remained the primary method of printing in China until the 19th century. It also provided the decisive foundation for the early spread of mechanically reproduced texts.

However, a closer inspection of the early examples of printing, which also furnished the basis for a rapidly flourishing book trade, reveals the fact that the oldest document of this kind came to us not from China but from North Korea. This document dates back to between 704 and 751 AD. Here, too, we are dealing with a religious text, a block print of Dharani-Sutra. But the famous Chinese block print of Diamond-Sutra, dating back to 868 A.D. is even more impressive. It contains a very beautiful woodcut representing the peak of a long period of artistic and technical endeavor. Today it is one of the priceless treasures of the British Museum.

The role which East Asia played in the development of the printed book was enhanced by China's development of paper-making techniques, in 105 A.D. and by the use of movable type by Pi Sheng in the middle of the 11th century A.D. Thus a broad base evolved for the development of a publishing industry and with it for a retail book trade. Fortunately we have access to a relatively large source of records relating to bookselling activity during this period. Throughout the centuries, that is, until the beginning of the technological era in the West many centuries later, bookselling was not subjected to significant fluctuations. It is worth noting that the techniques of printing played a role in this.

True, the Chinese knew the use of movable type, but they never reached the point of Gutenberg's invention of type casting. In view of the huge numbers of characters in the Chinese alphabet, Pi Sheng's ingenious idea was abandoned in favor of block printing.

Let us look at the early texts as they relate to the selling of books. Two publications, *The Invention of Printing In China and Its Spread Westward* by T. F. Carter and L. C. Goodrich (New York 1955) and Ming-Sun Poon's article in *The Library* (Chicago 1973) contain much information to which we will refer.

It is obvious that in the early Chinese period Buddhist monks sold manuscripts, which they had copied, to the public. A link appears to have existed with India, according to a Chinese Buddhist pilgrim who lived in India at the end of the 7th century. He left us a description of how priests as well as laymen created the image of Buddha out of mud from which they made prints. This leads us to inquire about the early stages of the art of printing in India. But since nothing has come down to us, except for this reference and a few other allusions, we can say little about this chapter of cultural history.

In the 7th century the forerunners of typographic prints were produced, but by the middle of the 9th century the manufacture and commercial exploitation of printed literature had become an established practice. This is revealed in a document according to which in December, 835 A.D. the official in charge submitted to the imperial household a proposal forbidding the printing of calendars from wood blocks. What is interesting about this

Figure 2. The earliest completely authentic reproduction of a bookstore that has been discovered up to now is from China and may be dated about 1100 A.D. This handsome scene shows a bookseller talking with a customer.

document is that these calendars were sold by local and traveling book dealers in the public squares. From another source of that period we learn that most of the book offerings at that time dealt with dream interpretation and geomancy or books on the nine celestial palaces, and the five planets, in addition to dictionaries and works on lexicography.

Other printers' notices clearly indicate that apart from an obviously widely scattered group of local and itinerant booksellers interested in more salable and popular literature, the China of that period had a very remarkable group of excellent bookshops catering to a demanding readership. It was the custom to address the book lover by assuring him that the editions offered for sale were the best of the best and by pointing out the quality of the particular kind of lettering. The item would be praised for the artistic merits of the illustrations. One of the publisher-booksellers even went so far as to insist that his offering would never find its equal in a thousand years. Some firms used fanciful names to attract attention ("Dragon Mount Bookstore"). Others stressed the virtues of a shop owned by the same family for generations. The location of the store was described at length with its address. There is documentary evidence pointing to the existence of printing, publishing and selling joined into one enterprise, as distinct from the independent retail book shop.

As can be seen we are dealing with book trade activities in all their forms, leading us to conclude that long before the beginning of European development, the Far East was familiar with problems of book trading which in some respects anticipated the challenges and difficulties of succeeding centuries. We have already alluded to the fact that the format of the Chinese book and the technique used to produce it underwent no substantial change for a number of centuries. It was not until China was opened to the West in the 19th century that the Celestial Empire entered a new era with the introduction of modern western printing methods which inevitably had a considerable influence on publishing as well as bookselling practices.

The centers of book activity at the turn of the millennium were Szechuan, the lower Yangtse Valley, and Loyang. Ming-Sun Poon in his study calls attention to the many colophons of the printed works of the Sung Dynasty (960–1279 A.D.) which shed considerable light on this period. A printer's note in a publication of the year 1152 A.D. contains an interesting, relatively early reference to the commercial activities of a house which combined printing, publishing, and bookselling. "We, the house of Yung Liu-lang, who were formerly located to the east of Grand Premier Temple of Eastern Capital are now temporarily lodging in the east of Wa-nan-Street of Lin-an prefectural seat, opening a bookstore for printing and distributing the classics, histories, etc. Presently, based on an old edition from the capital, we collated and published this book, the core text of Pao Pu-tzu. Surely, the text is free from even a single error. Inquisitive gentlemen from four directions who collect books please bestow your elegant attention. Written on 1st day of the 6th month in the 22nd year of Shao-hsing." (1152)

The existence even then of problems in connection with assembling an inventory of books of quality is revealed in another colophon dated 1191. "Many have grieved over the fact that good editions of Kung-yang and Ku-liang traditions have not been available in the bookstores. Based on my family-owned Academy edition, I collated with the other Chiang-nan and Che-kiang local government editions and made many corrections. But the characters in phonetic annotations by Master Lu sometimes differ from those in the text proper.... Controversies over the text have been plentiful, and I dare not alter any part of it according to my own humble judgement. For the time being I have preserved both readings to await the learned. In the mid-Winter of the 2nd year of Shao-hsi written by Yü Jen-chung of Chien-an."

Most recently, political developments have created changes with the nationalization and centralization of the entire book industry. The traditionally independent retail bookseller is now a division of a centralized system. We have to look to Taiwan for a link to the traditional methods of the once privately owned Chinese retail book trade.

Regrettably a number of booksellers in Taipei have earned a dubious reputation by printing and distributing pirated texts. As we have already mentioned, the earliest example in existence is a woodblock from Korea dating back to the first half of the 8th century A.D. We know that the book trade of that country developed its own character relatively early. This was the case especially after the 10th century when the establishment of national colleges for higher learning and numerous pedagogical institutions created a favorable climate for such a development. This trend was nurtured by the invention in 1235 of Korean typecasting, a method far superior to that of the Chinese, which was to have a far-reaching influence on the book trade. Nevertheless, block printing survived in spite of this innovation. Its importance to the book trade derived from its application in the printing of folklore which along with other writings enjoyed considerable popularity after the Korean alphabetization in the 17th century following the introduction of an easily acquired alphabet.

When in the middle of the last century Korea became accessible to the western world a new situation arose affecting publishing and bookselling in many ways. Bookselling, like publishing, developed along western lines. Later the restrictions imposed on booksellers as a result of the Japanese occupation in 1905 created severe obstacles for the trade. It was only after the country's liberation in 1945 that a basis for an active and liberal book trade could be created.

In *Japan*, too, we find printed documents of a very early era. Reproduced on woodblocks, Buddhist incantations reflecting the influence of the Chinese and Korean examples can be traced to the 8th century. Several copies of an impression of this kind of which presumably a million copies were printed, are still in existence.

Activities relating to the book trade of that time and for centuries after were carried on by the Buddhist monasteries, with the old imperial towns of Nara and Kyoto as centers. At this early stage the literature consisted chiefly of religious texts. As in China and Korea books and texts were mostly produced by block printing into the 18th and 19th centuries, even though letter presses were known in Japan as early as the 16th century. During a military invasion of Korea, Japanese troops came upon native print shops using movable type. Whatever they could cart away they brought back to Japan. This, aided by the printing offices established by the Jesuits (1580–1611), became the starting point of modern printing methods in Japan.

There is ample evidence that the Edo period (1600–1867) in Japan enjoyed a flourishing book trade. In many respects its traditional character has been preserved to this day. At the same time the influence of the western world is unmistakable. It can be traced to the middle of the past century. The end of World War II in 1945 brought many changes in antiquated concepts that had governed the book trade. Thus, the Japanese book trade of today combines modern practices with the best of Japan's traditional past.

Little is known about the history of the book in India prior to the 16th century. Most probably the documents which would give us our insight into the earliest history of books became victims of the severe climate in that part of the world. The account of a Chinese traveler in the 7th century, mentioned

Figure 3. Many pictorial examples of the early Japanese book trade have been preserved. Here a Japanese artist, Katsushika Hokusai, in a woodcut from 1799, portrays a store in Edo (later Tokyo) specializing in books and prints. The inscriptions in this handsome print show at the top the name of the store, to the right a listing of some of the latest books and in the foreground on the small column the name of the proprietor and the street address of the store.

earlier, gives us some idea of the status of books before the introduction of the art of printing.

The establishment of a Jesuit press in Goa in 1515 marked the beginning of a new, well-documented era. In the course of time other missionary presses followed and ultimately government or private printing establishments came into being. There are ample sources to prove how intensively the book trade was involved in the distribution of all of these publications. They not only served to satisfy the demands of colonials and western institutions but more important, catered to the native educational needs through translations into the Indian languages, an achievement for which the missions deserve most of the credit.

However, it was not until the liberation from the colonial yoke that retail bookselling came of age and began to serve the nation. It has since then become a strong factor in the cultural and economic life, although still suffering from the handicaps stemming from the diversity of languages, the country's economic difficulties, and the extended links of communications, not to mention other vexing problems.

We are obliged to limit ourselves to these few examples relating to Asia. This is not to ignore the relatively early and active existence of a book trade in countries such as Burma, Ceylon, Indonesia, Singapore, and Thailand, which are typical of other countries we cannot include for lack of space.

Europe

As mentioned before, the earliest documents relating to books known to mankind originated in classical Greece and ancient Rome. It was only then that the book trade, although exclusively confined to codices and scrolls, assumed certain forms which can be considered the forerunners of the burgeoning book trade of the West. To this extent we can speak of a European book tradition dating back to the 5th century, B.C., a tradition which developed unevenly until the fall of Rome, and which even thereafter left its mark on the realm of books of the later Christian era in Europe.

We know from ancient Greek sources that the copying of private texts was a custom, even in antiquity. Plato, Euripides, and Aristophanes among others mention this in their writings. It is doubtful that copies thus produced were traded commercially, at least we find no proof of this until the second half of the 5th century B.C. The term "bookdealer" appeared at that time with the designation of "βιβλιοπωλγς" which eventually became the Latin "bibliopola". There is considerable source material shedding light on the book trade practices of that age.

Aristophanes in *The Birds* speaks of the Athenian who immediately after breakfast rushes off to the books—meaning bookmarket—to find out about the latest offerings. Socrates too has provided us with similar references which all point to the transformation from the originally private endeavors of copying to the existence of literary and philosophical work designed for more general use. This provided the basis for a flourishing book trade within a relatively short span of time.

The expanding dominance of Greece in the Mediterranean and the spread of Greek thought through the civilized world of that era lent further impetus to the growth of bookselling. Thus, beginning with the 4th century B.C., we find increasing evidence of an expanding book trade, which the founding and growth of large libraries in Alexandria and the existence of the magnificent libraries of Greek Asia Minor, notably in Pergamon and Ephesus, provided additional momentum to the development. Parenthetically we might mention that the famous library in Alexandria had not always acquired its treasures by peaceful or commercial means. There was a flourishing practice of copying within the library, nor did one recoil from resorting to criminal methods in the procurement of books. It is common knowledge that foreign vessels putting in to Alexandria were subjected to search for the purpose of confiscating books which then were added to the library's inventory. The bibliomania of the age of Ptolemy knew no bounds.

Strangely enough no pictorial material relating to the book trade in ancient Greece has come down to us. On the other hand we have many illustrations depicting persons reading or writing and busy with the scrolls in use at that time.

In ancient Rome book trade activities reflected the influence of Greek example. But they also revealed new components, thanks to a flourishing Latin literature and also because of Rome's pragmatic sense for what was practical and attainable. Records from the pre-Christian centuries bear witness to this trend. Whatever we can scan from the Greek records about book trade practices is more graphically revealed in the samples of Roman literature. Suddenly the story of the book from its beginning to its distribution becomes alive and with that our evolved theme, i.e. book distribution, appears in a new light.

The student of classical literature will recall that Cicero's friend Titus Pomponius Atticus (110–32 B.C.) was both his publisher and bookseller. The correspondence between the two is most illuminating especially on this point.

The family of booksellers called Sosius became even more famous. They took care of the works of Horace who in his epistles speaks of the fate of his writings. A poem of great interest to our subject begins as follows:

Vortumnum Ianumque, liber, spectare videris,
scilicet ut prostes sosiorum pumice mundus;
odisti clavis et grata sigilla pudico,
paucis ostendi gemis et communia laudas,
non ita nutritus: fuge quo descendere gestis.
non erit emisso reditus tibi.

Book of mine, I know why you're looking wistfully
Towards the gates of Janus and Vortumnus.
So impatient are you to be in the market place, all decked
    out
In new finery and on display by the brothers Sosius.
The time is past when you could hide yourself inside my
    desk
So coyly and discreetly from the public gaze.
You hate confinement, you are panting to be free,
You fret when only a few are aware that you exist.
That's not the way I brought you up. But since that is what
    you want,
Go where your fancy beckons. Soon enough you'll be sorry.
But then it will be too late. Once you are out there,
You can't ever come back.

(English translation by Charles B. Anderson)

Horace describes how his book casts a furtive glance at Janus, in a passageway leading to the Forum in which merchants, as well as booksellers, were installed. At the same time the volume keeps an eye on Vortumnus, the god of merchants, whose statue stood in front of the bookshop section of Rome. His work was on display in the shop of the Sosius family hoping to accomplish its assignment, namely, to get it into the hands of an eager customer. The poet speaks of his inescapable compulsion, at the same time wondering whether the ultimate fate of the book will justify it.

The skepticism which Horace harbored toward the readers of his time is eloquently expressed further in these words:

> What, will you say, book of mine, when someone does you harm, when the reader crumples you because he has had enough of you? What will become of you when youth has forsaken you: When you begin to look shop-worn after being thumbed by the hands of the vulgar. Either you will feed the barbarous moths in silence, or fly to Utica or to Ilerda. But perhaps under the rays of a milder sun you may still find a reader to whom you may speak about your author?

To this Horace adds a few self-appreciatory remarks, boasting of his great accomplishments despite his humble origin. He depicts himself as one of small stature, prematurely gray and quick to fly into a rage, and to become as quickly pacified.

There are other names among the booksellers of ancient Rome, such as Tryphon and Secundus. The writings of Martial and Quintilian provide further information about the booksellers of the time, their problems and their social position. In response to a friend's request to give him one of his books, Martial suggests his going to Tryphon the bookseller, to which his friend counters that he is not prepared to spend money for it since book begging has always been part of our cultural heritage.

Martial refers to this again in another poem. He voices his disapproval of a request of a friend who had sent his servant to borrow his latest book of epigrams. Martial counsels him to abstain, suggesting how tiresome it would be to climb all the stairs to see him. Would it not be much simpler, he asks, if his friend when next at the Argiletum would pay the bookstore a visit? He will find signs filled with announcements of new books, which will give him a complete overview of all the books carried in stock. There at the bookstore run by Atrectus he might ask for Martial's epigrams. They are to be found on the first and second shelves and may be obtained for 5 denarii.

As can be seen, the book trade of ancient Rome was far flung and extended into far-away areas dominated by Rome. Horace's quotation bears this out. Other sources reflect the extraordinary internationality of bookselling at that time. Poets boast how their works are read throughout the world and Ovid, exiled to the Black Sea, finds consolation in the thought that he has a following throughout the Roman Empire. It is also noteworthy that ancient Rome enjoyed a second-hand book trade which extended to all parts of the Empire.

The Middle Ages

The book trade of the Middle Ages was essentially confined to the monasteries. Many of them maintained scriptoria, writing rooms devoted to the copying, lettering and illuminating of manuscripts. It would be misleading to refer to this as a phase of the book trade. But there exists documentary evidence suggesting that the number of scrolls thus prepared was frequently in excess of monastic requirements and in such cases resulted in the swapping of scrolls or selling of manuscripts.

The growing economic and cultural importance of European towns in the late Middle Ages gave birth to writing rooms of a more mundane and commercial kind. They certainly can be considered as an early form of publishing and bookselling, and in a sense can be considered a distant parallel to the scriptoria of antiquity, especially of Rome. The best examples of this are the "stationarii" of the University of Paris.

Writing rooms for the general public are a matter of record. The most famous one was that of Diebold Lauber in Hagenau in the Alsace, which from 1427 to 1460 conducted a regular and documented book business. Certain professions connected with the making of books began to establish themselves as recognized businesses in the larger towns of that time, as for instance the parchment makers and bookbinders.

❡ Mors refecat/mors omne necat quod carne creatur   ❡ Nobiliū tenet imperiū nulli reueretur
   Magnificos premit ꝛ modicos/cunctis dominatur.   Tam ducibus ꝗ principiꝰ cōmunis habetur.

❡ Nunc vbi ius/vbi fey/vbi voy/vbi flos iuuenilis.hic nisi pus/nisi fey/nisi terre precio vilis.

    ❡ Le mort   ❡ Le mort

❡ Venez danser vng tourdion   ❡ Sus auant vous ires apres
Imprimeurs sus legierement   Maistre libraire marchez auant
Venez tost/pour conclusion   Vous me regardez de bien pres
Mourir vous fault certainement   Laissez voz liures maintenant
Faictes vng fault habillement   Danser vous fault/a quel galant
Presses/ꝛ capses vous fault laisser   Mettez icy vostre pensee
Reculer ny fault nullement   Comment vous reculez marchant
A souurage on congnoist souurier.   Cōmencement nest pas fusee

    ❡ Les imprimeurs   ❡ Le libraire

❡ Helas ou aurons nous recours   ❡ Me fault il maulgre moy danser
Puis que la mort nous espie   Je croy que ouy/mozt me presse
Imprime auons tous les cours   Et me contrainct de me auancer
De la saincte theologie   Nesse pas dure destresse
Loix decret/ꝛ poeterie/   Mes liures il fault que ie laisse
Par nr̄e art plusieurs font grans clers   Et ma boutique desormais
Reseuee en est clergie   Dont ie pers toute lyesse
Les vouloirs des gens font diuers   Tel est blece qui ney peult mais.

                                                  6

Figure 4. Except for an illustration with a description in English handwriting of the 14th century that may or may not have specific reference to the book trade, the plate above, from La Grant Danse Macabre, *published by M. Husz in Lyon in 1499, is regarded as the earliest pictorial example of a European bookstore. At the same time it is the first woodcut of this kind preserved to us. In this picture we follow the progress of the book from typesetting, through printing, and then into the bookstore itself. In the presence of Death, who is reaching out his hand to the bookseller, the latter bemoans the fact that he must leave behind his books and his store and so renounce all the joys of his life.*

Germany

Johann Gutenberg and his invention of type casting (1438–1450), the basis of printing from movable type signaled the beginning of a new era, which provided the foundation for the birth and growth of publishing as we know it today.

Figure 5. Another handsome relic in the iconography of the retail book trade is this print from Venice in the year 1533. Used by Johannes Romberch to illustrate his work Congestorium artificiose memorie, *it is the first authentic example which shows the exterior of a European bookstore. Below the sign Bibliopola (from the Greek through Latin meaning bookseller), the shop has a show window with an impressive display of books.*

The significance of this extraordinary invention, which technically and aesthetically far exceeded the earlier East Asian efforts and which culminated in the Bible of 42 line pages printed under the direction of Gutenberg, was also reflected in the rapid spread of printing and publishing in Europe.

Beginning with Mainz as the first printing center in the western hemisphere, we have records of presses existing in Strasbourg in 1460, in Subiaco near Rome in 1465, in Rome in 1467, in Venice in 1469, and in Basel, Paris and Utrecht in 1470. By 1500 Gutenberg's invention had spread to 247 European towns. All told, by the turn of the century some 40,000 titles had been published in millions of copies. The threshold of the modern age had been crossed.

Obviously the work of Johann Gutenberg first led to the rapid development and spread of the book trade in the German countries of that day. The functions of printer, publisher, and bookseller were combined into one trade. But slowly the divergent tasks of each of the three branches led to a separation, at first with the divorce of printing from publishing and bookselling. The commonality of these two great branches for a long time after played an important role in the history of the book trade, not only in Germany but wherever German was spoken.

The end of the 18th century and the beginning of the 19th century witnessed the beginning of a trend which finally resulted in an autonomous publishing industry and an independent network of retailers. This is still essentially true for West Germany, with only a few exceptions where the bookseller is also a publisher. The traditionally proven collaboration between these two branches is reflected in the fact that with almost no exception the publishers distribute their own books exclusively through retail outlets. The relatively early existence of a structure based on the interdependence among publishers, wholesalers, and retailers played an important part in creating the architecture for a trade organization to serve the entire book industry. The German Publishers and Booksellers Association as a trade organization has served as a model for many other European countries. The policy of bringing all branches of the book trade together to discuss problems of mutual concern remains a basic policy of the organization.

This is the guiding philosophy of the Börsenverein des

Figure 6. Itinerant booksellers at all times and on every continent have played an important part in the dissemination of the printed word. They have been known, like some other members of the great bookseller family, to have a fondness for the bottle and at times to imbibe too freely. This weakness caught the fancy of Jost Amman, who exploited it for the design of a deck of playing cards produced in Nuremberg in 1588. Tipsy from too much sweet wine, our good bookseller has fallen asleep on the roadside. The monkeys, without any awareness of proper decorum, have taken advantage of his condition to play all kinds of tricks on him. In the accompanying text the bookseller is described thus: "When sober he could strike fear in the heart of a lion, now, however, he has become the laughing stock of the monkeys."

Figure 7. Even as late as the 17th century it was customary for books to be displayed with unbound pages so that buyers might select their own binding. This picture shows the interior of a bookstore in the first half of the 17th century.

Figure 8. We know from a whole series of illustrations and also from various references in literature that it was the custom in the early years of the European book trade to ship books mostly in casks or barrels. This seemed to be the easiest and surest way of transporting books for long distances over rough country roads. This print by Jan Luyken from Regensburg, Germany in 1698 shows books being packed for shipment.

deutschen Buchhandels in Frankfurt. Following the division of Germany into West and East Germany it represents the liberal tradition of the German book trade. The Börsenverein der deutschen Buchhändler of East Germany, located in Leipzig, is backed by a more or less nationalized book industry committed to conformity and patterned after the trade organization of the Soviet Union. There are roughly 4000 bookshops in existence in West Germany representing a ratio of one store to 10,000 inhabitants. Each year the international influence of the West German book industry is reflected in the Frankfurt Book Fair, the largest and most influential of its kind.

France

The history of the French book trade is firmly rooted in the Sorbonne. Centuries before Gutenberg, the "Stationarii" of the Paris university fulfilled the functions of publisher and bookseller of scrolls. When the Sorbonne licensed the use of the first press, printing spread like wildfire. At the turn of the 16th century, printing presses, publishers, and booksellers were active in some forty towns in France.

The fame of France as the leading cultural country from the 18th century on proved a boost to the development of the book trade. Its center, of course, was Paris, but the French provinces,

Figure 9. By the middle of the 17th century the bookstore had become a meeting place for men and women of letters and of high society, as this illustration, one of a series by Abraham Bosse, plainly shows. It depicts a bookstand in the Galerie du Palais in Paris about 1640 and amid all the elaborate ornamentation there are signs overhead and on the shelves indicating subject categories and individual titles. This plate also has value for scholars interested in the reading habits of the 17th century.

too, provided the climate for a brisk book trade which, aided by the use of the French language as a means of international communication, spread beyond the country's frontiers. Nevertheless, the lustre of this brilliant period was greatly dimmed by censorship with all its odiousness. Alongside authors and publishers numerous booksellers are known to have supported the progressive ideas of the French Revolution.

France clung to the corporate fusion of publisher-bookseller longer than her neighbors to the East. Even today we find a number of firms combining these two functions, in addition to a large group of independent retailers. The great tradition has served them in good stead. Nevertheless the adjustment to the rapid change of the times and new demands by the buying public have caused certain problems. One of the most essential challenges is the need to apply modern methods of distribution to the territories outside Paris. We should not conclude this chapter without mentioning France's struggle for price protection as a legacy of the past.

Great Britain

It makes a considerable difference from which vantage point one appraises the milestones of bookselling in Great Britain. To a varying degree British book trade methods exerted an influence throughout the world. Obviously this holds true for the erstwhile colonies, but British methods also had an effect on countries which had achieved national independence comparatively early, such as the United States. A survey of the history of the New World as well as of Asia, Africa, and Australia reveals the strong influence which radiated from the United Kingdom. A case in point is the attractive bookshop in Accra (Ghana) called "The Atlas Book Shop." It embodies a tradition based on a London bookshop of the 17th century which did business "under the sign of the Atlas." Its owner, Joseph Noxon, is still remembered as the author of a masterly work "Mechanick Exercises on the Whole Art of Printing" (1683–1689), in its time the most famous instructional manual on composition and printing. The bookshop in Accra is owned by one of Noxon's descendants. This serves as an

Figure 10. In the 18th century in many of those countries which could even then look back on a long "bookish" tradition, there were lending libraries and reading rooms which were almost always linked to the retail book trade and are therefore an important part of its history. We have a good many examples of stores of this kind, like the copperplate, left, from the catalog of a bookseller in Zürich in 1777.

example of the relationship with the homeland and spotlights the tradition of the British book trade.

The fascinating history of the structure of the overseas book trade under British rule is of a scope that defies description. Strangely enough the historians have paid scant attention to this colorful chapter in the history of the book.

Let us briefly examine some of the facts that characterize the history of the book trade in the United Kingdom. As it concerns the printed book, it started with William Caxton, Britain's first printer, in 1476. As was the custom of that age almost everywhere, the functions of printing, publishing and selling were combined in one endeavor. Parallel to the development in other parts of Europe, the turn of the 19th century witnessed a growing divergence of the three branches of the book industry, although the division between publishing and selling was not as

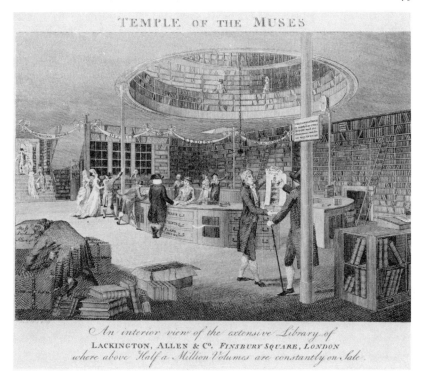

TEMPLE OF THE MUSES

An interior view of the extensive Library of
LACKINGTON, ALLEN & Cº. FINSBURY SQUARE, LONDON
where above Half a Million Volumes are constantly on Sale.

Figure 11. One of the most interesting and amusing characters of the retail British book trade was James Lackington, who was a bookseller in the last part of the 18th century and the beginning of the 19th and who, among other autobiographical data, has left us a book of memoirs called The First Forty Years of the Life of James Lackington. *Founder of a spectacular bookstore which he called with considerable justification "The Temple of the Muses," he was one of the most colorful booksellers in the history of the trade.*

pronounced as in Central Europe. There are still a fairly large number of publishing houses in Great Britain managing their own book outlets. We should not fail to mention the influential role played by the Stationers' Company in 1534, the earliest form of the British book trade. Its strict regulations, which included complicated ownership conditions, left their mark on British retail practices into the second half of the 17th century.

One of the outstanding achievements of the British retail book trade was the installation of reading and lending libraries. Their early versions served as forerunners of public libraries in the 18th century. This gave rise to a development which in the opinion of many today contributed to the struggle of British booksellers, since more books are borrowed from libraries than bought in bookshops.

Another achievement of considerable importance was the stand taken by British booksellers on the subject of the Net Book System. This with the cooperation of British publishers created a firm foundation for a successful retail book trade, by no means free of problems nor immune to criticism. There remain two formidable challenges, first, the creation of an improved training program for booksellers and second, the implementation of a more efficient system of distribution. Actually these are two

Figure 12. Bookstores for children and young adults are no phenomenon of our time. In the first half of the 19th century there were booksellers who specialized in books for children and who truly offered a large and far-ranging selection, as this handsome picture, supposedly from Nuremberg in the first half of the 19th century, bears witness.

Figure 13. Throughout the 19th century more and more booksellers became specialists in one field or another and chose fixturing and tables which best served the purpose of their specialty. The wood engraving, left, is from the middle of the 19th century and shows a store which specialized in scholarly scientific books.

problems with which the book trade throughout the world is grappling today.

Spain

The history of the Spanish book trade has its beginning with the introduction of the art of printing by German printers. We do not know the exact date of their arrival on the Iberian Peninsula, but it probably took place between 1470 and 1477. The Spanish book trade has had a varied history. Undoubtedly, the spread of Spanish books to overseas territories, which during their dependency relied on Spain for their supply of books, proved important in the development of the Spanish book trade. A less encouraging, even restrictive element, was the official censorship which existed for many centuries. An old encyclopedia (J.F. Krunitz, *Oeconomische Encyclopädie* T 1.7 Berlin 1776) records the following:

> In Spain a book has to be cleared by six courts before its publication can be announced.
> 1. Whereupon it is examined by the synodical examiner of the archbishopric at the request of the vicar.
> 2. Whereupon it is remanded to the Courts clerk of the kingdom to be recorded in the Chronista de Castilla, Aragon, Valencia.
> 3. Whereupon if sanctioned by him, permission is granted by the vicar and attested to by a notary.
> 4. Whereupon a letter of franchise must be obtained from His Majesty signed by a secretary.
> 5. Whereupon it is printed and sent to the Corrector general por Su Majestad who compares it with the copy signed by the vicar, lest something has been added or changed.
> 6. Whereupon the gentlemen of the Grand Council will decide for how much unbound copies may be sold.

Nevertheless in 1833 Spain adopted a more liberal point of view towards the printed word and in so doing encouraged the growth of a modern publishing and book trade business, as evidenced by the flowering of the book industry in Madrid and Barcelona, for example, which to this day remain the dominant centers of the Spanish book industry. Although Spain as a result of the Civil War lost many of its prominent publishers who established themselves successfully in the Spanish speaking countries of Latin America, it has recently renewed old international connections in the book trade. This has benefited the retail bookseller in Spain who incidentally is often affiliated with a publishing house.

Russia and the Soviet Union

We know that the Russian printer, publisher and bookseller, Ivan Federov, began his work in 1564, the year that the first samples of his work are dated. The growth of the Russian book trade including bookselling was hampered by severe difficulties. The most obvious was the censorship which made itself felt everywhere, while the low level of education also kept the book trade within narrow limits. Under a later, more liberal Czarist regime there was an improvement in this condition. During that period publishing firms, their names deserving to be inscribed in the annals of Russian history, came into existence. Some of them were domestic enterprises while others were managed by foreign interests attracted by a strong demand for French or German literature.

The Russian Revolution of 1917 broke with all tradition including that of the book trade. This not only applied to Russia but occurred in other parts of the world when the Communists took over. At first hesitantly, then with growing intensity, the entire book industry became nationalized. Private publishers and booksellers became government officials. What formerly was accomplished through personal competence, dedication and farsightedness became part of a social and political function. Within the limits of its governmental structure the Soviets can boast of impressive accomplishments thanks to their efforts to stamp out illiteracy and the formation of an efficient network for the distribution of books. The significance of this transformation which began in 1917 lies in the fact that after World War II many countries in East and Southeast Europe, as well as Red China, North Korea, North Vietnam, and in Cuba made the Soviet book system the basis of their own trade structure. Thus, for the first time in the world history of the book trade two

basically different systems are competing with each other. The outcome of this confrontation is being closely observed by the developing countries engaged in the establishment of their own publishing system.

Latin America

The history of the American book trade is divided into the pre-Columbian period and the age of discovery and conquest of the New World. For obvious reasons we are obliged to focus on the second part, however not before reminding the reader of the rich tradition of scroll writing in existence before the discovery of America about which there exists a wealth of important documents. However, we find no proof of any book trade activity involving manuscripts connected with the classical culture of the pre-Columbian Indian.

The drive by the Spaniards for expansion led to the introduction of the art of printing in the New World, presumably in 1535 in Mexico City. Other South and Central American countries followed suit. The output of these printer-publishers consisted mostly of religious writings, which also formed the bulk of the relatively sizable importation from the Spanish motherland. Accordingly the scope of activities of the bookseller was greatly restricted. It was only in the course of the movement for independence and the struggle for liberation resulting in the emergence of Sovereign Latin-American nations that the stage was set for an expansion. The surge in retail bookselling in Central and South America began with the 19th century and was given impetus by European booksellers who had come to the New World to start a new existence. We need only refer to that large group of able and farseeing Spaniards who as the result of the Civil War instilled new vitality into the book trade of Central and South America. Nor should we forget the numerous emigrants who left Germany in the years between 1933 and 1945, to make a single contribution on an international scale to the book industry in this part of the world. The political events of the world in this century served more than ever to strengthen the independent structure of the book trade in Central and

South America. The publishers and booksellers in a number of the Latin American countries are quite on a par with those in Spain.

The United States

Printing presses and the book played an important role from the beginning of the colonization of the North American continent. The political events in the New World emanating from the strong, individual beliefs of the immigrants living in more or less isolated communities, assigned a key role to the book trade. Its influence was more far-reaching than in the case of the Spanish and Portuguese colonists who had to contend with the censors of a central government. Once again, we are dealing here with fundamental differences which promoted the rapid development of the book trade and the creation of a free nation.

The introduction of the printing press in the United States by Stephen Day in 1639 in Cambridge, Massachusetts, was an event of historical importance. It would seem redundant to stress its significance to the American reader. The rapid development of printing, producing an abundance of material in addition to the voluminous importation of books from England, enabled a prospering retail trade to offer an imposing selection of books, all things considered. It reflected the spiritual and religious climate which gave such strength to the drive for liberty.

As early as the close of the 18th century printing presses, publishing houses, and booksellers conducted their business in twenty-four states. The role played by itinerant booksellers in the opening of the West, as well as by those who set up stores, forms an important chapter in the history of American bookselling. And yet it remains unrecorded. This points up another void in the existing histories dealing with the book trade. While there is a wealth of material relating to our subject—historical works, treatises and articles—the United States, too, has thus far failed to produce a history of its own book trade. If we leaf through the documents we are struck by the role which some outstanding booksellers played in the intellectual world of an early era and by the extent with which they fostered the noble and progressive aims of the young nation. We find examples in Boston, later in

Figure 14. Pictured above is the famous Old Corner Book Store in Boston, dated about 1835. The building itself was erected as a residence in 1711 and in 1828 was renovated to house the bookstore. The Old Corner was one of the meeting places of the great literary men of the time, such as Hawthorne, Emerson, Thoreau, Parkinson, and many others.

Philadelphia, and finally in New York. Outstanding booksellers are still to be found throughout the country.

In proportion to its population the number of booksellers in the United States is smaller than in the European countries with a long literary tradition. But through their work a great tradition

Figure 15. The penetration of the Far West, the great migration of America across the Mississippi and the Missouri over the rolling plains to the Rocky Mountains and the Pacific, has been responsible for a number of contributions to bookseller iconography. A good example is the picture above of King's Book Store in Shasta, California, which appeared on a letterhead in San Francisco in 1851.

Figure 16. While the bookstores that were being set up at this time in the pioneer West were often hardly worthy of the name, there were stores in the East that were large and spectacular, like this one in Boston in 1854. A description written at the time to accompany the picture runs as follows: "The representation gives a view of an establishment which may be considered a model bookstore. It is in length one hundred forty feet, twenty feet wide, and fourteen feet high. It is beautifully lighted not only by the large plate glass windows in front, but also in the rear by two large skylights, so that the entire store, notwithstanding its great depth, is as light as any small store. The arrangement of the store, as regards its shelving, position of counters etc. strikes us as being most admirable."

has been endowed with vitality and strength in an age of communication explosion and the towering predominance of bestsellers.

Canada

Much that has been said about the early existence of the North American book trade holds true for Canada. Admittedly, there are differences resulting from the two languages spoken in that country. For a while, because of the overwhelming presence of books from the United States the problem of establishing an independent Canadian press remained mostly below the surface. More recently, these problems have made their presence felt. It is to be hoped that the outcome will be a help to the retail bookseller in his struggle for excellence and versatility and his devotion to candor throughout the world and to the preservation of thought.

Africa

In the few articles that have been written about the history of the printed book in Africa, it is customary to date the start of the book trade there as 1798, the year when the first printing press was brought to Capetown. When we examine the facts more closely, we find that there were printers in Africa before this time. We have documentary evidence that Jewish artisans must be regarded as the first actual printers on the continent when they set up presses in Fez, Morocco, in 1521–1522 and later in Cairo in 1557.

Furthermore there may well have been, at the time of the last crusades, printers using block prints to produce texts of the Koran. At any rate this is the conjecture of Carter and Goodrich in *The Invention of Printing and Its Spread Westward,* in which the authors devote a section to "Block Printing in the Period of the Crusades." As evidence they refer to the block prints discovered by the Austrian Archduke Rainer in El Fayum and preserved today in the Austrian National Library in Vienna. Up to this time, unfortunately, no thoroughgoing study of these documents has been made by modern scholars.

If we go back further into old Egypt of classical times, it is conceivable that the extensive production of handwritten papyruses for the dead may have led to a form of bookselling. We have papyrus scrolls in which the names of the dead persons are in a handwriting different from that of the text itself. This suggests that the scrolls were finished in quantity and then sold. But for want of specific source material to prove it, this theory must be regarded as conjectural.

We are doing the history of the modern African book trade no injustice if we place its beginning at the end of the 18th century and the start of the 19th. It was from that time on that missionary societies were chiefly responsible for what was accomplished. In most cases it was they who set up the first printing presses and often under the most trying circumstances, produced and distributed religious tracts and translations of the Bible. More than that, these societies must often be credited with being the first publishers and sellers of books of a nonreligious nature. This is a great historical accomplishment deserving our lasting respect, since in almost every case it led to writing and printing in the native African languages.

In the former African colonial territories—meaning, of course, almost all of Africa—some retail bookstores were set up by the English, French and Spanish in the 19th century and more in the 20th. Some of these were really exemplary bookstores, although except for works of a religious nature, the books offered for sale were almost entirely in English, French and Spanish and not in the native African languages.

As the African nations first acquired independence, they began to work towards the development of their own African traditions. Though economic and linguistic factors greatly complicate the task, they are proceeding apace in the cultivation of what is their own heritage. For the future we may assume that many more large and impressive bookstores in addition to those already existing, will be set up. Besides these, the international type of bookstores with their emphasis on a wide selection of imported books will be retained and these stores will make their contribution to the independent African life.

It should be added that as early as the middle of the last century the book trade in the countries of northern Africa where Arabic is spoken had already been taking on independent characteristics, influenced to be sure, by the French language and culture.

Australia

In the book *Australian Bookselling* by Roger Page published in 1970, there is a chapter concerned with the history of the trade "down under" that has been most helpful for the purposes of this survey. From it we learn that the first bona fide Australian bookstore was started in 1828. Before that time, as early as 1803, books had been sold through newspaper agencies. The first "full-time" Australian bookseller also had the distinction of having published the first book catalogue. Issued in 1829, it was entitled "A catalogue of books in the circulating library of William McGarvie." So we have to do here with a store that offered books both for sale and for rent, a custom inherited from the English mother country. The Australian booksellers have indeed always been influenced by the traditions of the British book trade, an influence which, though it persists even today, has diminished as the native trade has become more and more self-reliant.

Until the Second World War the books offered for sale in Australian bookstores were practically all imported from London. Today Australian booksellers order and stock many titles from the United States. And as Australian publishers in increasing numbers have been producing books of quality on many subjects, local booksellers are becoming less dependent in general on imported books.

New Zealand

In 1835 the Church Missionary Society set up the first printing press in New Zealand and was responsible shortly thereafter for developing an active book trade. It is interesting to note that this same organization also produced and distributed books in Maori, the language of the aborigines of the country. But even today the best bookstores are chiefly dependent on imported books, which they get from Great Britain, Australia and the United States.

Bibliography

INTRODUCTION

W. T. Berg and H. C. Poole, *Annals of Printing.* London 1966.

C. Clair, *A Chronology of Printing.* London 1969.
>   (Although both the books above are chiefly concerned with the
>   history of printing, there are also historical references to the
>   book trade.)

S. Taubert, *Bibliopola.* 2 vols. New York 1966. (Pictures and texts about
>   the book trade.)

S. Taubert (ed.), *The Book Trade of the World.* 3 vols. New York 1972–
>   1976. (Along with concise historical information from all coun-
>   tries of the world there are descriptions of the present-day
>   conditions of the book trade; also an extensive bibliography of
>   all branches of the trade, past and present.)

H.D.L. Vervliet (ed.), *Liber Librorum.* London 1972. (Published on the
>   occasion of International Book Year, proclaimed by Unesco in
>   1972, it is a far-reaching summary of 5,000 years in the history
>   and art of the book. Many international experts cooperated in
>   its production. With bibliographical references.)

CHINA

T. F. Carter and L. C. Goodrich, *The Invention of Printing in China and
>   Its Spread Westward.* 2nd ed. New York 1955.

Chang Ching-Lu, (Source Materials for the History of the Modern
>   Chinese Publishing Industry.) 4 vols. with supplement. Peking
>   1954–59. In Chinese.

Chin-Tang Lo, *The Evolution of Chinese Books.* Taipei c. 1960.

D. Kaser, *Book Pirating in Taiwan.* Philadelphia 1969.

Ming-Sun Poon, "The Printer's Colophon in Sung China, 960–1279."
>   *The Library Quarterly,* vol. 43, number 1, pp. 39–52, Chicago
>   1973.

G. R. Nunn, *Publishing in Mainland China.* Cambridge, Mass. 1966.

T. H. Tsien, *Written on Bamboo and Silk.* Chicago 1962.

KOREA

Books and National Development. Seoul 1968.

Pow-Key Sohn, *Early Korean Typography.* Seoul 1971.

JAPAN

M. Hashimoto, *Nihon Shuppan Hanbai Shi.* (History of the Japanese Book Trade). Tokyo 1964. In Japanese.

H. Higuchi and A. Haruhlko, *Kyoho Igo Edo Shuppan Shomoku.* (A Catalogue of Books Published in the Period After 1716). Toyohashi 1962. In Japanese.

K. Kawase, *Gozamban No Kenkyu.* (Bibliographical Study of the Gozamban Editions of Medieval Japan, 1200–1500.) Tokyo 1970. In Japanese.

K. Kawase, *Heiancho Surikyo No Kenkyu.* (Printing of Buddhist Texts in the Heian Period.) Tokyo 1940. In Japanese.

K. Kawase, *Kokatsuji-ban No Kenkyu.* (Study of the Early Typographic Editions of Japan.) Tokyo 1967. In Japanese.

INDIA

K. S. Diehl, *Early Indian Imprints.* New York 1964.

D. N. Malhotra (ed.), *Book Development* (in India). New Delhi 1969.

A. K. Priolkar, *The Printing Press in India, Its Beginning and Early Development.* Bombay 1958.

D. E. Rhodes, *The Spread of Printing: India, Pakistan, Ceylon, Burma and Thailand.* Amsterdam 1969.

ANCIENT GREECE AND ROME

F. G. Kenyon, *Books and Readers in Ancient Greece and Rome.* 2nd ed. Oxford 1951.

T. Kleberg, *Bokhandel och Bokforlag i Antiken.* (Retail Book Trade and Publishing in Classical Greece and Rome.) Stockholm 1962. In Swedish. German edition under the title *Buchhandel und Verlagswesen in der Antike.* Darmstadt 1967. Bibliography pp. 208–212.

W. Schubert, *Das Buch bei den Griechen und Römern.* (The Book among the Greeks and Romans.) 3rd ed. Heidelberg 1962.

H. Widmann, *Herstellung und Vertrieb des Buches in der Griechisch-römischen Welt.* (Production and Distribution of Books in Greece and Rome.) Archiv für Geschichte des Buchwesens, VII. Frankfurt am Main 1967.

THE MIDDLE AGES

F. Geldner, *Die Deutschen Inkunabeldrucker.* (German Printers Before
1500.) 2 vols. Stuttgart 1968–70.

O. Hase, *Die Koberger.* 2nd ed. Leipzig 1885.

H. Lulfing, *Johannes Gutenberg und das Buchwesen des 14. und 15. Jahrhun-
derts.* Leipzig 1969.

G. H. Putnam, *Books and Their Makers During the Middle Ages.* 2 vols. New
York 1896–1897. Reprinted New York 1962.

S. H. Steinberg, *Five Hundred Years of Printing.* Harmondsworth 1955.

S. Taubert, *The Book Trade of the World.* Vol. 1: *International Section and
Europe.* Hamburg, London, New York 1972.

GERMANY

F. Kapp and J. Goldfriedrich, *Geschichte des deutschen Buchhandels.* (History of the German Book Trade.) 4 vols. and Index. Leipzig
1886–1923.

H. Widmann, *Geschichte des Buchhandels vom Altertum bis zur Gegenwart.*
(History of the Book Trade from Antiquity to the Present.)
Wiesbaden 1952.

H. Widmann, H. Kliemann and B. Wendt, *Der deutsche Buchhandel in
Urkunden und Quellen.* (The German Book Trade, Documents
and Source Material.) 2 vols. Hamburg 1965.

FRANCE

M. Chavardes, *Histoire de la librairie.* (History of the Book Trade.) Paris
1967.

L. Febvre and H. J. Martin, *L'Apparition du livre.* (The Appearance of
the Book.) Paris 1955.

H. J. Martin, *Histoire du livre.* (History of the Book.) 2 vols. Paris 1964.

J. A. Néret, *Histoire illustrée de la librairie et du livre français.* (Illustrated
History of the Book Trade and of the French Book.) Paris 1953.

GREAT BRITAIN

R. E. Barker and G. R. Davies, *Books Are Different. An Account of the Defence
of the Net Book Agreement.* London 1968.

H. S. Bennett, *English Books and Readers 1475 to 1557.* 2nd ed. London
1969.

H. S. Bennett, *English Books and Readers 1558 to 1603.* London 1969.

H. S. Bennett, *English Books and Readers 1603 to 1640.* London 1970.

H. Curwen, *A History of Booksellers.* London 1873. Republished 1969 (Detroit).

R. Myers, *The British Book Trade from Caxton to the Present Day. A Bibliographical Guide.* London 1973.

F. A. Mumby and I. Norris, *Publishing and Bookselling.* 5th ed. London 1974.

M. Plant, *The English Book Trade.* 2nd ed. London 1965.

W. Roberts, *The Earlier History of English Bookselling.* London 1889. Republished 1967 (Detroit).

SPAIN

P. Bohigas, *El Libro Español.* (The Spanish Book.) Barcelona 1962.

J. Madurell Marimon and J. Rudio y Balague (eds.), *Documentos para la historia de la imprenta y libreria en Barcelona 1474–1553.* (Documents about the History of the Book Trade in Barcelona.) Barcelona 1955.

S. Olives Canals, "Un Centenario: Conferencia de editores españoles y amigos del libro el año 1917 en Barcelona" (A Centennial; Meeting of Spanish Publishers and Friends of the Book in Barcelona in 1917.) *El Libro español,* October issue 1967.

P. Vindel, *El Libro español, su labor cultural y bibliográfica en España desde el siglo XV hasta nuestros días.* (The Spanish Book, Its Cultural and Bibliographical Influence in Spain from the Fifteenth Century to the Present Time.) Madrid 1934.

RUSSIA

M. V. Muratov, *Kniznoje delo v Rossii v 19 i 20 Vekach.* (The Book Trade in Russia in the 19th and 20th Centuries.) An essay on the history of book publishing and book marketing, 1800–1917.) Moscow and Leningrad 1931.

Organizacija i Technika Torgovli Knigoj. (The Book Trade, Organization and Techniques.) Moscow 1969.

Pecat SSR. (USSR Publication, Statistics.) Moscow. An Annual.

L. Y. Rabin and A. N. Lyubimo, *Ekonomika i Plairovanie Torgovli Knigami.* (Book Trade Economy and Planning.) Moscow 1968.

LATIN AMERICA

L. S. Thompson, *Printing in Colonial Spanish America.* Hamden, Conn. 1962.

Hans Biedermann, *Altmexicos Heilige Bücher.* (Old Mexico's Holy
  Books.) Graz 1971.

THE UNITED STATES

The Bowker Annual of Library and Book Trade Information. New York and
  London.
O. H. Cheney, *Economic Survey of the Book Industry, 1930–1931.* New
  York 1931.
C. B. Grannis (ed.), *What Happens in Book Publishing?* 2nd ed. New York.
E. Harman, *The University as Publisher.* Toronto 1961.
C. Kerr, *A Report on American University Presses.* Chapel Hill 1949.
H. Lehmann-Haupt, *The Book in America.* New York 1951.
W. Miller, *The Book Industry.* New York 1949.
F. L. Schick, *The Paperbound Book in America.* New York 1958.
J. Tebbel, *A History of Book Publishing in the United States.* 3 vols. New
  York 1972–1976.

CANADA

*Royal Commission on Book Publishing: Canadian Publishers and Canadian
  Publishing.* Toronto 1973.

AFRICA

A. H. Smith, *The Spread of Printing: South Africa.* Amsterdam 1971.
S. Taubert (ed.), *African Book Trade Directory 1971.* Munich and New
  York 1971.

AUSTRALIA AND NEW ZEALAND

D. H. Borchardt, *The Spread of Printing: Australia.* Amsterdam 1969.
F. Macmillan, *The Spread of Printing: New Zealand.* Amsterdam 1969.
R. Page, *Australian Bookselling.* London 1970.

III

More Than Merchants: Seventy-Five Years of the ABA

by *Chandler B. Grannis*

formerly editor-in-chief *Publishers Weekly*

Most good booksellers take satisfaction both in their effectiveness as merchants and in something beyond that: their function
in bringing books to people, serving their communities as centers of entertainment, information and culture. Similarly, the
American Booksellers Association can take pride in its record
both as an effective business organization and as a vital aid to
the entire world of books.

Here is a most remarkable trade organization. It is remarkable
for its durability; there has never been any question of that. In
its early years the ABA depended upon the dedicated efforts of
a relatively few people, and its continuing durability is a natural
result of its leadership. It is one of the nation's oldest trade
associations in point of continuous operation and support.

From the very beginning, ABA officers, boards of trade and
directors have represented in an unbroken line some of the most
capable men and women in book retailing. This leadership has
come from all parts of the country and from the different kinds
of bookselling. Many of these people have been outstanding
personalities—and, virtually all, not only successful in their own
work, but willing to donate time, talent and money in the service
of all American booksellers and therefore of the whole industry.

With able and persistent leadership and a sense of cohesion
among members, the ABA has proved able to change with the
times. ABA meetings and activities have mirrored the cultural
trends and public events of 75 years. The organization has
grown both in size and in even more important ways. For what

emerges from a look at the ABA's history is a story of growth from largely parochial—though utterly vital—concerns to a concern for industry-wide relationships; from concentration on the plague of price-cutting to a focus on methods of selling; from simple, traditional modes of operation to sophisticated management techniques and merchandising. It is a story of the growth

State Street near Washington in Chicago about 1870. The several bookstores side by side were known as Booksellers' Row.

of professionalism, a development in attitudes and skills which determined the growth of the association, and which changed, and continues to change, the face of bookselling in America.

The American Booksellers Association came into being after exactly a century of failed efforts to form some coherent, lasting organization of the retail book trade.[1] Its nearest predecessor, the American Book-Trade Association, had been set up in 1874, but neither the leaders' vigor nor the trade's willingness to work for a common, sustained program was sufficient under the chaotic conditions of the era. The ABTA fell into silence and ceased activity after three years.

Heart of the Matter: Net Prices

Almost a quarter-century later a new generation of bookmen—and some old hands, newly hopeful—made, under new conditions, a new try. In the nation at large, the economic robber barons and their political allies were being challenged, and reform was beginning to sweeten the air. In the book world, publishers had reached a stronger consensus than ever before about the need for stability in prices and distribution and were ready to form their own organization. Across the sea, the book trade of Great Britain, bedeviled by under-selling as were the Americans, tried out and then established in 1899 a net-price system: sellers who violated "net" or "fair" (publishers' specified minimum) prices, were cut off from supplies. The British example heartened American booksellers and publishers.

If the ABA has a single, distinct anniversary date it is probably November 15, 1900—as the late book industry historian, John T. Winterich, pointed out in his delightful account written for the ABA's 50th anniversary book.[2] It was on that day that an organizing committee of six booksellers sent out a letter to the trade, in the name of an organization they were forming, to be called the American Booksellers Association.

[1]See preceding chapter by John Tebbel.
[2]"The First Half-Century of the ABA" by John T. Winterich in *ABA Almanac 1950.* American Booksellers Association, New York. 1950.

Chairman of the committee was Charles W. Burrows of Burrows Brothers, Cleveland; members were W. Millard Palmer of Lyon, Kymer & Palmer, Grand Rapids, Michigan; Clarence W. Sanders of St. Paul (Minnesota) Book & Stationery; William T. Smith of Utica, New York; Albert C. Walker of Scrantom, Wetmore, Rochester, New York; and, as secretary, John W. Nichols, formerly of Harper & Brothers' educational department. In March 1901 they announced completion of organization plans, and called a convention for July 24, in New York City, at the Earlington Hotel, 55 West 27th Street (reservations $1.50 a day, "two beds in a large room, with bath").

All the arrangements had been made by Mr. Nichols, "to whom," reported *Publishers' Weekly,* March 30, 1901, "the credit for forming the Association is so largely due." *PW* added: "The plan of organization is far-reaching and carefully thought out." Part of the plan called for local and state associations "in harmony with the suggestion of the Publishers Association," so as to facilitate application of the net price plan. Signing up 748 booksellers as members, at dues of $2 a year, the founding group formed an advisory board of 50, representing all states except North Dakota, and named Henry T. Coates of Philadelphia as president, with Secretary Nichols as manager, at a small fee. In May the organization issued, for booksellers to give to patrons, a pamphlet about net prices, showing that the net price plan was meant to bring about "a one-price system," which would mean "a fair price" to the purchaser.

Meanwhile, leading publishers had formed, early in the year, the American Publishers Association, and had agreed, effective May 1, to establish net prices on such books "as the individual publisher may desire" (excluding schoolbooks, adult fiction, and new editions), and to sell them only to booksellers who would maintain those net prices for a year.

Soon came the ABA's first convention, with much discussion of price-cutters and the meaning of net prices, and a banquet boldly billed as "first annual"; the ABA founders clearly intended their association to endure. The Convention voted full support for the net price plan, but they insisted that it ought to cover fiction. Some booksellers, in fact, had told the ABA they would not join until fiction was protected. At any rate, in a resoundingly named "Reform Resolution No. 1," the ABA members agreed not to deal with publishers who declined to join in the net price plan; not to supply any dealer denounced by the publisher as a violator; and to expel violators from the ABA.

Banquet festivities at that first convention took the form of 16 toasts, which, while doubtless warming (in Manhattan in late July without air conditioning), had serious intent. The subjects as listed in the elegantly printed banquet program were: The Bookseller and the Librarian. The Middle West. The Two Big B's—Books and Boston. The Net Price System. The Western Publisher. Bookselling as a Profession. The Bookseller in New England. Net Books on the Pacific Coast. Books in the Department Store. The Greek Lamp in the West. (At this point the score was West 3, New England 2.) Local Associations. The Bookseller in the Sunny South. What Profits It? The Things We Hope For. The New York Booksellers Association. The Secretary.

At the 1902 Convention, held at New York's Herald Square Hotel 11 months later, the ABA's second president, Clarence E. Wolcott of Wolcott & West, Syracuse, New York, said the net price system should be extended beyond its initial limited range to cover new copyright fiction (new "serious" books being already protected); and the purchaser's discount on fiction should be limited to 10%. But he felt that in the first year of the ABA it was important simply to have checked the downward tendency in book prices (as against list prices, he meant), and to have brought about some harmony within the trade.

It was in 1902, also, that a session with distinguished authors was for the first time a feature of the ABA convention, thanks to a publisher's hospitality. Colonel George M. Harvey, the managerial dynamo who had become head of Harper & Brothers, invited the convention—about 60 men—to visit its pressroom, there "to see the actual manufacture of books" and to hear informal remarks by Mark Twain (he appeared again in 1908 as banquet speaker), William Dean Howells, John Kendrick Bangs and Hamlin Garland. The remarks consisted of rather ponderous banter, and were not memorable except that they marked a mutual recognition of the interlocking interests of author, publisher and bookseller.

It was in this same year that the net price system received its great challenge, a suit against the publishers by R. H. Macy & Co. to restrain them from boycotting non-complying retailers. The case was to drag on from appeal to counter-appeal for 12 years, until the U.S. Supreme Court ruled against the publishers and awarded damages of $150,000 to Macy's.

The long litigation and the defeat did not end the application of the net price idea in one form or another, and in fact the fight for price stability provided the booksellers for many years with a unifying theme under the ABA.

As always, a few active members worked hard for the many. Although membership by 1904 had reached 850, only a relatively small number of booksellers contributed in 1905 to cover the deficit caused by ABA's share in the repeated litigations.

Convention attendance jumped up and down a good deal. After good initial turnouts, attendance was down to 36 in 1907, and then moved up: 59 in 1908, 88 in 1909, 254 in 1911, 294 in 1912. (Membership was to fluctuate widely for decades; in one Depression year, 1934, it was about half the 1904 figure.)

Pressure for a higher level of net prices was continuous. The 1906 convention celebrated publishers' granting of a two-year term for price protection, but called for a net price of $1.20 on $1.50 fiction. The call was repeated in 1907 and 1908 and 1909, since publishers persisted—though they gave in eventually—in holding a net price of $1.08. This price was "absurd," according to one bookseller, because it made it "necessary to keep a customer waiting while he (the bookseller) goes to the back of the store to get the two cents change." The price was still absurd when the $1.50 novel was pegged net at $1.12, since, as W. B. Clarke of Boston reminded the 1908 assemblage, the $1.50 novel cost the dealer 90 cents, so the gross profit was 22 cents, but the cost of doing business was 28 cents; result, a loss of 6 cents. The 1907 session called for a publishers' discount of one-third off list—a demand that was still being pressed at the 1913 convention.

Turn Towards Wider Interests

Booksellers' interests were not quite as narrow as the endless reports of price and discount discussion might suggest. They expressed concern over ABA members who were victims of the San Francisco earthquake and fire in 1906. They kept up their program of sedate entertainment at annual meetings. In 1907, for example, they visited the Doubleday, Page plant, met the discoverer of the North Pole, Commander Robert E. Peary, and were regaled at their banquet by the "Purple Cow" poet, Gelett Burgess, presented by his young publisher, Ben W. Huebsch. Meantime, some members were feeling concern—to quote a *PW* editorial, May 18, 1907—that only "an old guard of 30 or 40 men" were devoting themselves to ABA. (*PW* hoped that "the 400 who have not as yet contributed their share to the support of the Association will be roused out of their torpor. . . .")

The most significant widening of concern was shown when the ABA began to talk about better sales methods, staff training, promotion, and good management. For example, in 1906 there was some discussion of circulating (i.e., rental) libraries, "novelties" (sidelines) and second-hand books, all as adjuncts to the selling of trade books. R. E. Sherwood, an ebullient young New York dealer, gave what was probably the ABA's first talk on innovative merchandising, with what *PW* called "an unvarnished account" of his "circus methods" of promotion. Perhaps these methods didn't catch on, for a year later one speaker was castigating the book trade for parochialism: "The bookseller is not in touch with the larger reading public."

There was progress, however, in another direction: in 1907 the first woman to hold a prominent place in ABA affairs, Mrs. Grace E. Going, was appointed office manager. Her salary was $6 a week.

The 1910 convention marked ABA's first strong emphasis on practical operations and selling techniques. The next year *PW* said that it was precisely because "net reform" had become a reality that booksellers could turn their main attention from the problems of buying to those of selling. President Walter L. Butler of Butler's, Wilmington, Del., reported what was on members' minds as they had written to him: the hope for price maintenance contracts; annoyance at publishers charging for postage; the need for uniform discounts on library sales. The next year, he said members were writing to him to express "a very positive conviction that the library business should be handled by the legitimate retail bookseller." Another 1912 speaker, a Doubleday executive, came up with a ringing new slogan—one that has been ringing ever since: "Fewer Books and Better."

At the 1913 meeting the ABA made an important and memorable move: it named a committee for a booksellers' school. This led to a New York course the next year "to improve the efficiency of booksellers' clerks," a course that the ABA held in cooperation with the Booksellers' League of New York; it was led by a young editor at the Century Company named Van Wyck Brooks. This was followed by a course in Philadelphia the next year, and by successive training programs, through the years, to be reviewed on a later page.

A lot had been said about returns in previous years, but it remained for W. H. Arnold of H. B. Claflin Co., New York City, to make in 1913 a concrete, practical proposal—a 90% returns system for books in stock one year. *PW* later said this plan was as important as the net price system. The 1913 meeting was important in still another way, for it voted to initiate a joint publisher-bookseller board of trade. This was the first of a long series of liaison groups. They have had varying life-spans, varying restrictions on subject matter, varying responses to the legal interpretations of the times, but they have been recognized as a vital necessity in trade relations.

Also considered in 1913 was the "reprint menace." John Kidd of Stewart, Kidd, Cincinnati, said reprints would not be so menacing if publishers would avoid issuing any low-cost reprint for three years after original publication.

The next several years confirmed ABA's breakaway from obsession with net price. Major attention in 1914 went to market expansion (83% of potential buyers of books had inadequate bookstore service or none, the ABA was told), and an address on "Bookselling as a Profession for Women" by Georgiana Hall of Wanamakers, a veteran "book salesman," as she expressed it in the semantics of the day. The next year, there was much talk of the potentials (and pitfalls) in cooperative advertising, and one landmark proposal, a plan for a "Juvenile Book Week" was presented by Franklin K. Mathiews, chief librarian of the Boy Scouts of America. Such considerations were followed up at the 1916 sessions, held in Chicago. (This was the first annual meeting outside of New York; more than half those present had never attended an ABA convention before, *PW* said.) At the 1917 meeting, "new channels" in bookselling—that is, specialized selling—were recognized. Several women managers of the new "personal" bookshops gave talks, and Bertha E. Mahoney of Boston's pioneering Bookshop for Boys and Girls led a stimulating discussion.

Meanwhile, beginning July 1916, the first *ABA Bulletin* was published for a couple of years in Detroit while Ward Macauley of that city was president of the ABA. The *Bulletin* stressed sales methods, service, price maintenance, and "a library in every home in America."

World War I and the Early Twenties

The book trade, like all the nation, was about to be caught up in World War I. Sympathy for the Allies ran high, and war books were selling briskly. The crusading element of America's short, decisive part in the war was reflected sharply in the 1918 convention rhetoric of President Macauley. He voiced the vast majority's consensus when he called the war "a conflict of ideals, democracy versus autocracy."

A new burst of energy marked the ABA's immediate postwar years. In 1919 the ABA's speakers included a veteran among publishers, Major George Haven Putnam; one of the younger breed of publishers, B. W. Huebsch; a young newspaper critic, Heywood Broun. Topics included postwar business opportunities, direct selling, library sales.

In 1920, postwar super-patriotism was calmly viewed in an International YMCA executive's talk on "Building Americanization Through Books"; he reminded listeners that "we are all immigrants." Meanwhile, ABA President Charles F. Butler demanded "fewer titles and better distribution," a dual goal almost as difficult to achieve as the deathless "fewer and better books."

Plans and programs continued to bubble, and at the 1921

convention in Atlantic City (*PW* gave 60 pages to the full proceedings!) Frederic G. Melcher, managing editor of *PW*, announced a plan for a "Year-Round Bookselling Campaign." This incorporated the new Children's Book Week but included also a promotion theme, with slogans and promotion materials, for each month in the year. But operating problems were not ignored: President Eugene L. Herr of Lancaster, Pennsylvania, acclaiming the 33 1/3% discount that had been secured from publishers "in recent years," said ABA studies had now "clearly shown that 36% was indispensable to the successful conduct of a retail business." And so, for several years, the ABA's battle cry in dealing with publishers was to be "One-third plus 5." The arithmetic was interesting; the idea was entirely clear.

In its first year, May 1921 to May 1922, the Year-'Round Bookselling Campaign was a center of attention. Sent out in this effort were "1,507,784 posters, circulars, circular letters and personal letters" to booksellers, librarians, churches, clubs, schools, magazines, newspapers and individuals. Meanwhile, experiments were being made with the bookmobile idea, and ABA secretary Belle Walker reported on the value of a "Book Caravan" to rural areas.

The ABA Goes Full-Time

All through the early 1920s, the need for a full-time staff executive with a broad program was becoming apparent. Under the prodding and enthusiasm of the energetic ABA President Walter V. McKee of Sheehan's, Detroit, the 1924 convention voted to create the post of executive secretary, and the board hired, to fill it, a young promotion man from Western Union, Ellis W. Meyers. He took on the job in time for the 1925 convention, and vigorously began lining up a program based on Mr. McKee's theme, "More and Better Bookselling"—a constructive switch on the old cliché. Mr. Meyers launched an "ABA Page" in *PW*, running several times a month on the average, with the magazine's cooperation. At the same time he resumed the publication of the monthly *ABA Bulletin.*

A big decision at the 25th annual celebration was to establish a Cooperative Clearing House to which booksellers sent their orders for New York publishers. At the Clearing House these orders were consolidated for shipment to the stores, thus saving substantial carriage costs. This service lasted until President Franklin D. Roosevelt in 1939 reduced the parcel post rate for books to 1 1/2 cents a pound, making the Clearing House unnecessary. An associated service, the Consolidated Warehouse (called American Booksellers Service Co.) was also set up and maintained until 1946. But one idea endorsed strongly in 1925 was never carried out—a proposal for a telegraph delivery service for books.

As Mr. Meyers described it in 1926, the kind of service given by the Clearing House illustrates the vast difference in scale between the industry of the 1920s and that of the 1970s. Each morning, New York publishers would pick up the orders that booksellers had mailed to the Clearing House; packages in fulfillment of these orders would go to the Clearing House that same afternoon. The Clearing House staff would then "enclose" each retailer's order from the different publishers' packages, and ship the books to the dealer in a single case of 100 to 150 pounds. (A 150–lb. case cost less than half the freight charge of five 35–lb. packages, Mr. Meyer said.) Shipment could be made the day after receipt of books from publishers, or two or three days' orders could be accumulated. Delivery in those days of complete railway service was prompt.

Cooperation with other organizations (on matters other than net price) had assumed a permanent place in ABA affairs by the mid-1920s. At the St. Louis Convention in 1926, publisher Ben Huebsch reported on the latest bookseller education program held in cooperation with the College of the City of New York, the Booksellers' League of New York, and Women's National Book Association[3]. (Pittsburgh booksellers held a course the following March, with 50 students.) Carl Milam, executive secretary of the American Library Association, cited the booksellers' mutual interest with the ALA in the latter's "Reading with a Purpose" promotion. The publishers, now organized, since 1920, in the National Association of Book Publishers, presented

[3]The League, formed in 1895, was an active local trade association in its early years, later mostly a social group; renamed, 1972, Book League of New York. The WNBA was formed November 13, 1917, in the Sunwise Turn bookshop, N.Y.C., as the Woman's National Association of the Booksellers and Publishers.

their joint promotion plans. "Books in Motion" was the slogan reported this time by the highly capable and resourceful NABP executive secretary, Marion Humble, a handsome lady whose romantic profile graced the *PW* convention reports each year in a different portrait.

Among 22 resolutions passed by the ABA in 1926, one was to incorporate the Association—partly to avoid personal liability in any legal judgments against the organization.

This was a convention at which the varied nature and differing problems of booksellers in different fields were recognized by the holding of eight round table sessions. They were for college stores[4]; religious stores; department store book sections; small town stores; children's departments or shops; large city stores; also for the consideration of bookstore accounting and finance, and of advertising, mail order and "special efforts."

The Book Club Battles Begin

As this historical sketch is prepared, the book clubs have been a fact of book distribution for almost 50 years. But shortly after ABA's 25th anniversary, they were brand new—and frightening. For several ensuing decades the clubs were primarily regarded by many leading booksellers as simply elaborate cut-rate mail-order schemes, unredeemed by their massive promotion of many titles. For at least a quarter-century the ABA fought them, through litigation and attempted competition, and still, in principle, opposes their price-cutting aspects. At the 1927 convention, Cedric R. Crowell of the Doubleday stores, argued that, while the Book-of-the-Month Club would stimulate the sale of particular titles, it would hurt the sale of books generally; that the Literary Guild policy of taking subscriptions through bookstores would injure normal store operations; and that the bookstores could offer better service than the clubs.

As a counter-move, the ABA tried in 1928 an elaborate "Bookselection Plan" under which the Association would obtain selected books from publishers at 55%, supply them to dealers

[4]Already, following informal talks at ABA meetings, bookstores in this field had formed in 1923 the College Bookstore Association, later the National Association of College Stores.

at discounts of 40% to 43%, and spend the difference on operating the plan and advertising the selections. The plan did not catch on—not enough, anyway, to sell the budgeted 10,000 books per three-month period. This despite a presumably savvy selection committee: booksellers Joseph A. Margolies and Marion Dodd, reviewer-editor Harry Hansen, authors Inez Havnes Irwin and Will Durant. Mainly because of the plan, the ABA by 1930 had a $17,500 deficit which it paid off by selling $25 debentures to booksellers; debenture holders waived their interest and most of the bonds were redeemed at a discount.

Promoting Promotion by Booksellers

Other ABA energies, fortunately, went into the encouragement of booksellers' own promotion. R. G. Montgomery of J. K. Gill's, Seattle, in 1927 told about "Making the Radio Sell Books for You," and Franklin Spier spoke on advertising, showing layouts of cooperative ads. The ABA made available to its members a series of ad mats featuring seasonal and gift themes. Their success was noted at the 1928 convention, when President John G. Kidd was also getting approval for a cooperative national ad campaign "to sell the bookshopping habit."

This was an expansive era for books; rental libraries were more and more popular, books were appearing as drugstore merchandise and selling by mail was increasing.

Along with these serious matters, and a full round of convention reports, how-to talks and special-interest round tables, the conventions of the 20s had their frisky moments. *PW* reported them faithfully (if not, perhaps, completely) under what became for a time an annual heading, "Playtime at the Convention"; play was apparently stimulated by Prohibition. An early highlight was the appearance of Harper's great salesman, Adam Burger, in the title role of a 1921 convention skit about the tribulations of bookselling, called "Eva, the Bookseller's Daughter." The 1927 sessions at New York's Hotel Commodore were enlivened by a carnival night from 10 P.M. to 2 A.M., and climaxed by a banquet where 1000 guests heard—among other celebrities—Will Durant, Bruce Barton, Henry Seidel Canby, and a repeated ABA performer and friend, Christopher Morley.

The precedent for today's celebrity parades at conventions was established.

Dual Conventions, East and West

Few remember it now, but for three consecutive years, 1929–1931, the ABA held two conventions: one on the West Coast, one in the East. They apparently were intended to be equal in status—but one of the two had to be the locus of formal business, and that was the Eastern meeting.

For the 1929 Western meeting, held in San Francisco, a strong team traveled from the East: Ellis Meyers and Marion

In October 1945 President Truman accepts ABA's gift of books to the White House Library. In the picture left to right are Rose Oller Harbaugh, ABA director; Isabel DuBois, director of Navy Libraries; Irita Van Doren, editor of the New York Herald Tribune Book Review; *Mrs. Truman; President Truman; Frederic G. Melcher, chairman and editor of* Publishers Weekly; *Joseph A. Margolies, ABA president; David C. Mearns of the Library of Congress; and Colonel Ray L. Trautman of the Army Library Service.*

Humble for the associations; Alfred Harcourt, J.W. Lippincott, and, with an inspirational message, Frederic G. Melcher, who said: "Great literature deserves great audiences, and if it is to reach the great audience of the Pacific slope adequately, there must be good marketing, too."

It was at this meeting that the idea of a home library for the White House, provided by the book trade, was first discussed. It had been suggested by Douglas A. Watson (a visitor to Herbert Hoover's White House) to the eminent San Francisco bookseller, John Howell. Howell brought the idea to the San Francisco convention. The delegates approved; so did those at the Eastern convention in Boston the next month. In 1930, 500 books were given by the trade to the White House. Since 1933, 200 representative new American books have been given every four years—with one shift in the schedule: no books were presented in the second Nixon Administration, but a presentation was made to President Ford in 1975.

The 1929 Boston convention also set another landmark: it authorized the Board of Trade to meet with a publishers' committee "to arrange for an intensive research into the Book Business in all its details," the various book trade groups to share the costs. This formalized the ABA's participation in the famous "Economic Survey of the Book Industry 1930–1931: Final Report by O.H. Cheney, Director," issued in 1931 by NABP (rev. ed., *Bowker,* 1949) and still valid in some of its observations about the disorderly nature of the book business.

Booksellers in The Depression

The Depression was now well on its misery-making way. Still the ABA was keeping up its services, even adding a monthly mailing piece for booksellers to distribute. In 1932 the ABA set up some 15 regional conferences to analyze "the merchandising principles" embodied in a considerable number of recommendations in the Cheney Report. Convention interest turned sharply towards budgets, cost control and renewed opposition to loss-leader selling. There was a lot of action, but the ABA had not only lost money on its Bookselection scheme; it was soon losing dues income as well. Ellis Meyers resigned early in 1933. His eight years of persistent initiative had been full of accomplishment, and he was missed. However, the basic ABA services were carried on by Robert M. Coles and another staff member, David T. Sachs. It was Bob Coles who then saw the ABA through the years of the National Recovery Administration (1933–1935) and into the war period.

The NRA was for the most part enthusiastically supported by the book trade. Booksellers, led by a group dubbed "The Three Musketeers" (Richard Fuller of the Old Corner, Boston, Frank Magel of the Putnam Bookstore, New York, and Cedric Crowell of the Doubleday Book Shops) lobbied for the inclusion of list-price maintenance, during some period in the life of a book, and other protective devices in the NRA Booksellers' Code. The ABA leaders sold NRA officials on the idea that such a code was needed for the survival of effective national bookstore service. Therefore a Supreme Court ruling against NRA—coming as it did during the ABA's 1935 meeting—was a shocker to the booksellers. *PW*'s headline, "Supreme Court Ruling Stuns Convention," was no exaggeration.

Nevertheless, the trade was now able to fall back upon a growing number of new state laws permitting producers (including publishers) of "labelled" competing products to write contracts with sellers requiring maintenance of minimum marked prices in the states having such laws. The federal Miller-Tydings Act made these contracts valid across state lines. The ABA vigorously backed this system—of which more, further on.

Essentially, however, the book trade was on its own; and the ABA continued to foster sales promotion activities. In 1936 the organization launched—at the suggestion of Virginia Kirkus— a plan called the National Book Award. It lasted until World War II, and unlike its later namesake, it was a set of awards bestowed by vote of all interested booksellers. Titles were selected as the "Booksellers' Favorite Novel," and nonfiction, and "Booksellers' Find" or "Discovery."

Association membership dipped during the Depression to much less than that of the ABA's first three or four years. As the Depression receded, membership began to recover: 507 member firms in all in 1937, 665 by 1941. ABA services were sustained and increased; an Order Blank Distribution Service (daily consolidation of orders mailed directly to ABA and hand-delivered to publishers) began in 1938; and in the same year, a Book Token plan, based on the successful British model, was adopted —later succeeded by the ABA's Give-a-Book Certificate plan. Also in 1938, the ABA began its long-lived New York Book-and-Author Luncheons. Promotion forums and special-interest round table group meetings marked the conventions of this period. The eventful 1938 sessions were remembered also for a trip up the Hudson to Sing Sing Prison in connection with a book by Warden Lewis E. Lawes. Exactly 201 booksellers entered the prison, and exactly 201 came out, *PW* reported with an air of relief.

The ABA in World War II

As World War II began in Europe, some of the great issues involved, particularly that of cultural freedom, were presented to ABA audiences by distinguished writers—Thomas Mann, refugee from Nazism; Carl Carmer, Sholem Asch, Drew Pearson, Carl Sandburg and others.

After December 7, 1941, the ABA again took its part in a national war effort. Karl Placht, president of ABA, telegraphed to President Roosevelt a full pledge of booksellers' cooperation. The ABA backed the Victory Book Campaign to collect 10 million books for the armed forces. Buy good books, the ABA urged the public; and when they are read, give them to the campaign, through library and bookstore collection points.

A committee under George Hecht of the Doubleday stores listed methods of conserving materials and reducing waste. Special issue-oriented booklists were drawn up. Speakers from Washington agencies explained new rules regarding materials. ABA was represented on the Council on Books in Wartime, which among other activities provided a flow of quality reading on many subjects, in pocket reprints, for the armed forces— almost 1200 titles and more than 123,000 copies. Archibald MacLeish urged the 1942 convention to start thinking of how books could help deal with postwar questions.

Meanwhile, book clerk training programs went on, and legislative questions, including the periodic problem of maintaining book post rates, were dealt with. An inspiring moment was pro-

April 23, 1942

To the American Booksellers Association:

I should have liked to be with you in person to extend my greetings and talk to you, for I have been a reader and buyer and borrower and collector of books all my life. It is more important that your work should go on now than it has ever been at any other time in our history: in a very literal sense you carry upon your bookshelves the light that guides civilization. I need not labor the contrast between the estate of books in the free democracies and the estate of books in the countries now brutalized by our foes.

We all know that books burn -- yet we have the greater knowledge that books cannot be killed by fire. People die, but books never die. No man and no force can abolish memory. No man and no force can put thought in a concentration camp forever. No man and no force can take from the world the books that embody man's eternal fight against tyranny of every kind. In this war, we know, books are weapons. And it is a part of your dedication always to make them weapons for man's freedom.

Franklin D. Roosevelt

vided by President Roosevelt's message to the 1942 convention, affirming the essentiality of books and of making them "weapons for man's freedom."

The projected 1943 convention was replaced by a New York business meeting and dinner (with a delegation of British publishers as guests); and a "convention in print" was held in the pages of *PW*. There were regional reports from members, reports on rationing and other wartime restrictions, and a demand that publishers give preference to established book outlets over short-term competitors who moved into books simply because their regular lines were in short supply. In 1944 a one-day convention took place. Honor was paid to Harcourt, Brace; Little, Brown; Morrow; and Norton for their consistently high standards of "business ethics in book distribution"—measured by their policies as to advertising, book club practices, efficiency, minimum discounts, price maintenance, fair practice in remaindering and reprinting, avoiding competition with booksellers, and not encouraging "new, unnatural accounts." The 1945 "convention" was again held "in print" and by mail; it consisted of replies to an extensive questionnaire on all the booksellers' problems. Results were reported by Harriet Anderson of the Channel Bookshop, New York, who from 1944 to mid-1946 carried on a wartime ABA Section in *PW*, replacing ABA's own *Bulletin.*

While Bob Coles was in the armed forces, his capable wife, the former Harriet Seligman, a member of the ABA staff, carried on in his stead. Mr. Coles, after his return, went to work for the Book-of-the-Month Club. Gilbert E. Goodkind, a young attorney who had worked with a New York City agency and later with the U.N. Relief and Rehabilitation Administration, was hired as executive secretary early in 1946.

Postwar Energies: Cooperation and Conflict

A big agenda had piled up during the war period. After 1945, many things happened fast. The ABA board decided early in 1946 to cut loose what had become a burden: it sold the American Booksellers Service Co., including the latter's principal activity, the Consolidated Warehouse. The purchaser was Barney

Lobell, who had been manager of the warehouse; he carried it on successfully as a private corporation. The ABA, while continuing the order distribution service, mat service, sale of book tokens, and sale of bookselling supplies, could now begin giving its energies to the meeting of new needs.

One of the needs was for a periodically issued *Basic Stock List*, and ABA President George A. Hecht of the Doubleday Book Shops headed up a committee to compile it. Another need was to assess the market ahead, and this was done at the first postwar convention, May, 1946, in New York; expansion was predicted, based on higher college enrollments, population growth, and new reading tastes developed in part by *Armed Services Editions.* A further need was to revive the monthly *ABA Bulletin,* which was done in July. The *Bulletin* continued until, in February, 1973, it was superseded by the weekly *ABA Newswire* as a regular means of communication. Now the *Bulletin* is reserved for discussion of specific information and appears sporadically.

In the fall of 1946, to help reestablish contacts broken during the war, the ABA set up six regional meetings, held in Chicago, San Francisco, Los Angeles, Dallas, Atlanta, and Philadelphia. The meetings gave members in these areas a chance to meet Mr. Goodkind and some of the new officers and to speak their minds.

The 1947 convention at the Hotel Astor in New York was in one way a very decisive one, for it introduced an informal trade show, called a "Buyers' Book Browse." It was the forerunner of the now formidable annual ABA Trade Exhibit. The ABA also announced a group insurance plan for members; revived the Joint Board of Booksellers and Publishers; started a new Gift Certificate Plan; and attained a membership of more than 1000 book retail firms. (The Joint Board did not last; worried about anti-trust considerations in 1949, the publishers terminated it.)

Meanwhile, some ideas put forward at the 1946 convention were percolating. Speakers at a major panel had insisted that the bookseller's problem was not competition from other bookstores; the main things needed were the enforcement of fair trade and the granting of higher discounts by publishers—40% on one copy being mentioned frequently. And new outlets should be encouraged; in a nation spottily supplied with bookstores, the presence of more well-managed stores would encourage more buying of books.

In line with this thinking, Mr. Hecht proposed that the ABA supply a "packaged bookstore"—standard plans, estimates, fixtures and basic stock for prospective book retailers. The packaged bookstore was first demonstrated at the 1948 convention in Chicago, along with display "assemblies" at various prices. This was the era when American store design was beginning its greatest revolution, and Doubleday's "modern," functional, colorful, self-service design was introducing a bright new look into the entire retail book trade.

Changes were obviously coming upon the trade, perhaps a bit too fast for easy adjustment. Mass market paperback lines, beginning to grow in number after the war, were becoming more interesting to general booksellers, but troubling, too, partly because of their low unit of sale, 25 cents. On the other hand, rising prices of hardcover trade books were also disturbing. Some listeners at the 1947 convention were unhappy when Bennett Cerf of Random House said bluntly that cost increases made the price hikes necessary.

Even less popular was Mr. Cerf's report that 40 to 50 leading publishers had found themselves dependent on subsidiary rights, and specifically on book club sales, for their profit margins. This was received rather badly in view of a revelation at the same meeting by ABA president Joseph A. Margolies of Brentano's, New York. Mr. Margolies reported that, by taking full advantage of book club offers, he could buy books from clubs at an overall sum below the cost of buying at publishers' wholesale prices.

Pricing and club problems were especially irritating in what seemed by 1948 to be "a tight market." The ABA's response, however, was not solely to lash out at enemies, but also to encourage more effective bookselling. Conventions now included very well-attended workshop meetings on better store operation—staff training, stock control, selective buying, and—a new point of emphasis at the 1949 meeting in Washington—the choice and handling of sidelines. At several meetings, successful ways of promoting and presenting children's books were featured, and in 1949, ABA president Robert B. Campbell reported progress on a basic booklist of children's titles.

Even though, on some issues, the ABA and publishers were at odds, cooperation was also going on. Mr. Hecht in 1948 proposed that publishers adopt in their advertising the slogan "Books Are Wonderful Gifts," to help lead customers into bookstores. This request was followed. At this time, too, the ABA was making one of its attempts to develop a uniform returns plan, and although publishers felt they could not join in a single policy, they cooperated to make possible a Returns Calendar, published in the *ABA Bulletin* from December 1948 until 1963.

Jubilee Year

Disputes over pricing practices and club policy did not keep the book trade from uniting in 1950 in a warm observance of the ABA's first half-century. The jubilee convention was held at the Hotel Astor in New York City, and there was no trade exhibit, its place being taken by publishers' ads in the anniversary book already mentioned. The convention focused more on the future than on the past. John O'Connor of Grosset & Dunlap told the assembled book people that a potential "vast expansion" of their market lay ahead, and explained the plan by the American Book Publishers Council to launch in 1951 a Committee on Reading Development to promote increased readership of books. Mr. O'Connor's news was welcome, especially since the ABA's first—admittedly limited—cost ratio survey, released at the convention, suggested that annual average bookstore profits ranged under 2%.

The jubilee convention included another brand-new subject, the ABA's first panel consideration of books and television. Speakers felt that while TV was yet another claimant for readers' time, it also offered new opportunities for promoting books and authors. A show of hands revealed that most booksellers present did not as yet have TV in their homes. A little later in the year the ABA made a survey of its members regarding the effects of television on their stores. They found that the experience of members "in television areas" of the then as yet unsaturated country compared with the experience of members on "non-television areas" showed that "the book trade's fear of television is unjustified" and the effect of TV on book sales was "absolutely nil." Today, of course, television is recognized as being, in many cases, a strong stimulus for book sales.

Price-Cutting and Fair Trade

The anniversary celebration was a pleasant break, but meanwhile the ABA was becoming increasingly angry about the book clubs' promotion of top-of-the-list books at cut-rate prices. Booksellers were able to cite specific instances of sales and customers lost to the clubs. ABA leaders asked why the booksellers should not be able to offer top titles to their customers at prices like those of the clubs.

Accordingly, in February, 1948, the association announced that it was asking publishers to lease to ABA the plates of certain books for reprinting and for sale at reduced prices. The publishers and books were: Houghton Mifflin, Churchill's *Memoirs*; Harper, Betty Smith's *Tomorrow Will Be Better*; Doubleday, Eisenhower's *Crusade in Europe*. The publishers said "No." Soon, all three books became major book club selections.

The ABA therefore complained to the Federal Trade Commission that the publishers were discriminating against booksellers in favor of the clubs. In mid-1949, while the FTC was investigating this claim, the ABA complained about alleged fair trade violations by the Dividend Book Club, and joined in a complaint by Burrows, Cleveland, that publishers were unfair in exempting book club selections from fair trade pricing. In February, 1951, the ABA joined Columbia Records' suit against the retailer, Sam Goody, for cutting prices on fair-traded records.

Meanwhile, the fair trade laws were being tested in other fields. In May, 1951, while the ABA was convening in Cleveland, the U.S. Supreme Court handed down a decision that laws binding nonsigners of fair trade contracts were not valid in interstate commerce. A wave of price-cutting broke out in many areas. This continued sporadically until, in July, 1953, a new federal law went into effect, the McGuire Act, again authorizing the interstate application of nonsigner provisions in state fair trade laws.

Two months after the May, 1951, Supreme Court decision,

there came an announcement by the FTC that it was issuing complaints against six publishers, charging them with, among other things, unfair discrimination in leasing plates exclusively to clubs, and in requiring retailers but not book clubs to honor fair trade prices. The publishers were Doubleday, Harper, Houghton Mifflin, Random House, Simon and Schuster, and Little, Brown. The ABA supplied witnesses to support these FTC charges, but opposed another item in the complaint, a challenge to the application of price contracts to nonsigners; the latter point, anyway, was dealt with by the McGuire Act. The full Federal Trade Commission in two decisions, 1953 and 1955, ruled that a publisher (the case had boiled down to Doubleday) could grant exclusive publishing rights to a book club under the publisher's copyright proprietorship; and because of "overriding public interest"; that the publisher must not *agree* with a club that it would require any bookseller to maintain minimum prices not required of the club; that the publisher must not discriminate in its prices to competing wholesalers; that books are in "free and open competition" and can be fair-traded.

For more than a decade after the McGuire Act was passed, violations of state fair trade laws were contested in the courts, and from 1958 to 1964 the ABA backed successive bills to strengthen price stability. But these bills failed to pass.

The rise of discount retailers throughout the country had spurred the ABA's support of such legislation. Conventions and regional meetings through the late 1950s and early 1960s produced loud cries against discounters. To a large extent, however, fair trade in the book industry has fallen into disuse in the decade up to this writing. The complaints at ABA meetings about price cutting diminished gradually (though never to the point of silence). Discount selling became, perhaps, more widespread than ever, but price-maintaining retailers seemed increasingly able to minimize its effects.

At several conventions, for example, some booksellers counselled their colleagues to do a little selective price-cutting of their own. The bookseller would thereby take away the discounter's principal advantage, while continuing to offer the professional bookseller's services: personalized attention, a well-trained staff with good knowledge of books and the local market, a comprehensive and varied or specialized stock, special-order handling, and other advantages not offered by the discounter or the sort of department store that ran a loss-leader book section with ephemeral stock and ill-informed clerks. The trained bookseller's displays of high-quality paperbacks, his remainder stock, and his special sales in the store and by mail could all strengthen his position when it came to price competition, it was pointed out in repeated ABA panels and workshops. The ABA's professional training and education programs were increasingly directed towards the kind of efficiency and merchandising that would make the serious book retailer less vulnerable to unfavorable conditions—including cut-rate competition. Moreover, it became increasingly arguable in the late 1960s and early 1970s that there was room for many different kinds of booksellers; specialists were finding their clienteles; the remainder chains had a useful function (and were selling most new titles at full price); and the established personal and professional booksellers were indispensable.

The most formidable price competition continued to come from the book clubs, and it was still not known how much—on balance—the club prices injured the bookstore sale of books offered by the clubs, and how much, on the other hand, the club promotion created sales in stores.

Figures and Economics

The ABA's 50th anniversary year survey of bookselling costs had elicited reports from only 133 firms, but it was indicative and useful. One thing it showed, Gilbert Goodkind pointed out in the summer of 1951, was that shipping costs averaged 1.9% of bookstore gross sales. The ABA board therefore was happy to thank Doubleday when that company announced in September that it was assuming all transportation charges to bookstores. Already the ABA had had some depressing reports at its convention in May. Bookstore mortality was up, Mr. Goodkind reported, and ABA membership had dropped from 1400 stores to 1370 in a year. During the convention, not only had the Supreme Court ruled against interstate fair trade, but the Interstate Commerce Commission had issued a ruling that had the effect of ending the special postal rate for books. Mr. Goodkind reminded members that the ABA had anticipated the postal decision by establishing in 1950 a Consolidated Shipping Service—not unlike the Clearing House of the 1920s. Fortunately in the autumn the U.S. Congress restored the book post rate and removed postage rates from ICC jurisdiction. The shipping plan was soon dropped.

Although the American Book Publishers Council had issued in 1951 a committee report thoroughly analyzing book trade problems, ABA leaders felt that publishers had done little about them. Many publishers, on the other hand, thought booksellers were making too many confusing demands. In the autumn of 1951, therefore, the ABA set up a Committee on Economic Aims to draw up minimum, presumably acceptable goals. The committee consisted of Ellsworth R. Young, Phillips' Book Store, Cambridge, Mass., chairman; Gordon W. Bryant, Lauriat's, Boston; John A. Reed, Langley's, Newton Centre, Mass.; and ABA President Allan McMahan, Lehman's, Ft. Wayne, Indiana.

Gilbert Goodkind was taking a major part in all these efforts and was earning strong respect throughout the industry. It was a grievous blow to all his associates when, on January 20, 1952, he was killed in an automobile accident while on vacation. Allan McMahan rallied the stunned staff to its many tasks, and Mr. Goodkind's chief aide, Dorothy McKenzie (later Jeltrup), was named acting executive secretary. In the spring Robert Pilpel was engaged as executive secretary, effective June 16, and served until the following March. His successor, as of July 1, 1953, was Joseph A. Duffy, for many years sales manager of successive publishing houses, and in 1950 director of the Ohio Book Project, an ABPC-sponsored, year-long study of a book market. Mr. Duffy's service to the ABA was to last until his death in 1972, embracing the ABA's period of most intense activity in its 75 years, and by far its greatest growth.

Two significant steps marked the ABA's activities as the year 1952 went on. First, the association named its first—and still its only—woman president, Marion Bacon, astute manager of the successful Vassar Cooperative Bookstore. Second, at the 1952 convention in Washington, Mr. Young and his committee on Economic Aims made their report.

They stated four goals: (1) full protection—with the store

assuming costs if returns became excessive; (2) carriage charges prepaid by the publisher; (3) minimum 2% cash discount; (4) formation of a "permanent and representative bookseller-publisher advisory body." These proposals were modest enough, in the light of the edge-of-disaster status of bookstores reported by Mr. McMahan at the convention: profits under 1% for "most retail bookstores." He had two long-range recommendations: development of regional book distribution centers to reduce delays and delivery costs; and establishment of a program to promote the reading habit—an effort to which the ABPC and the new (1954) National Book Committee would soon address themselves.

Some publishers soon complied with one or more of the ABA's "Economic Aims," though, after a year, the committee felt progress was still slow. The publishers asked for a list of practices that seemed to the bookstores to cause unnecessary expense. The ABA responded with "A Bill of Particulars" giving detailed recommendations for "the elimination of waste" in six areas: billing procedure; shipping and packing; returns; special orders; transportation costs; jackets and mailings. The ABA and the ABPC's Book Distribution Committee separately wrote comments and action proposals for each heading, and the full report was given out and discussed during the 1953 Chicago convention.

A year later, convening in Atlantic City, the ABA took up another economic question, the effects of publishers' subsidiary rights—book club, serial, and paperback rights—upon bookstores. Publishers and booksellers took predictably opposing views, but no one disputed Harold Guinzburg of Viking when he said that the potential markets were far greater than all parts of the industry together were meeting.

In 1955 the ABA attempted a second cost-ratio survey, and enough stores reported to show figures for stores doing under $50,000 annual sales and those doing over $50,000. The smaller firms had stock costs of 61.4%, operating costs of 36.8%, and profit before taxes of 2.4%; for the larger stores, the figures were 64.7%, 31.6% and 4.3% respectively. For both, average stock turnover was 3.3 times. Few stores, if any, were rolling in wealth. Nevertheless, ABA and *Publishers Weekly* polls of bookstores showed healthy annual increases in sales—often 10% and

12%—in the late 1950s and early 1960s. In 1959, President Charles B. Anderson of Anderson's, Larchmont, N.Y., strongly called the membership's notice to the widening opportunities for booksellers because of growth in population, education, and shopping center development, then in its infancy. New opportunities underlined, he said, the need for greater professionalism in store management.

In 1961 the ABA leaders were saying that the economic aims they had sought were largely still to be achieved. In this year, however, the ABA set up for the first time an enduring mechanism for liaison with publishers—its own Goodwill Committee of leading booksellers to call upon individual publishers for informal talks on problems of mutual interest. To encourage and show adequate appreciation to publishers who performed the best all-round service in supplying the stores, the ABA set up a Publisher of the Year Award, and made the first presentation at the 1964 convention. The next year, following the death of John Barnes of Barnes & Noble, publisher-bookseller, a second award for superior service was introduced and both were presented until 1970, as the John Barnes Awards.

At the 1961 convention some very serious speakers looked into the possible economic and social picture of the 1960s. John Gardner, author of "Excellence" (*Harper*), later founder of Common Cause, argued that the potential for books lay in the development of a habit of "lifelong learning" among increasing numbers of people. A McGraw-Hill economist foresaw certain market trends which later proved to affect the content of books and the approaches of the people who marketed them: the importance of youth under 30 and of the new feminine majority; more leisure time; more consumer spending; more direct mail selling. He did not, of course, foresee the Vietnam War, with its disruptive effects soon to be felt in college and general bookstores in varied and complex ways.

Long-range issues concerned most delegates to the 1961 convention less than practical matters did. Some members complained anew about clubs, paperback supply services, discount outlets' competition, and publishers' mail directly competing with the same publishers' outlets.

One perennial practical issue—delay in delivery—was examined statistically in 1965 by James M. Kobak, then of the J. K.

Lasser accounting firm. While one aspect of his report stressed the need for better cost controls, its most vital point was the growing gap between receipt of an order in a publishing house and the arrival of the books at the store. There were regional variations in these delays, and variations in publishers' performance, but on the whole, the periods of delivery were to lengthen rather than to shorten during the decade that followed. One major reason for this seemed to be that relatively few publishers had fully mastered the new technology used in order fulfillment.

In 1968 the ABA sponsored an intensive study of bookstore economics by the accounting firm of Ernst & Ernst. Their report was entitled "Success Factors in Bookselling." It identified these factors, including financial controls, and indicated that a third of the booksellers examined were "unprofitable" at the time. The following year, Roysce Smith, then of the Yale Co-op, pointed out that even the "successful" shops had "dangerously low" profit margins. To this problem the ABA has continued to address its programs by emphasizing methods for stores to improve their own profitability.

Management and Merchandising

As the ABA looked increasingly into the trade's economic condition in the 50s and 60s, it accordingly gave growing attention to the management and merchandising techniques that might alleviate that condition. It continued also to try out a variety of services directed to the same purpose.

An *ABA Bulletin* page in September, 1951, listed some of those services—some later terminated after becoming outdated, and a few still in effect: The Returns Calendar, no longer needed by 1963, when most publishers had ceased setting specific dates for returns; the Order Distribution Service, long useful, but too cumbersome and costly to keep up after publishers moved their order fulfillment divisions out of Manhattan; wrapping materials; display fixtures; advertising mats; general information provided by letter or telephone; the hardbound and paperback *Basic Book Lists;* Give-a-Book Certificates (at this time redeemable at any member store, but later simplified for sale and redemption at a single store only); the indispensable *ABA Book Buyers' Handbook* (which during Mr. Duffy's years at the helm of ABA developed into a comprehensive, encyclopedic, looseleaf volume revised annually; and lists of publishers' mailing pieces and pre-pub and other special offers.)

For many years the *Bulletin* included occasional instructional articles by experts—information on taxes, invoices, special orders, rental libraries, sidelines and many more topics. Mailed with the *Bulletin* were advance versions of numerous chapters written for the first edition of the *Manual on Bookselling*. (See *Education for Bookselling* p. 105.) The evolution of the *Bulletin* in February, 1973, into the *ABA Newswire*, featuring schedules of author appearances and major book reviews, plus essential news, is familiar to ABA members and friends. Additional management tools continuing today include *Basic Book Lists*, in alternate years, of hardbound and paperbound books; the *Sidelines Directory*, started in 1955, most recently revised in 1974; and a *Bookstore Staff Manual*, 1953, also revised in 1974.

The handling of special orders was a problem for both publishers and booksellers. In order to speed service and reduce costs to both publishers and booksellers, discussion between ABA and ABPC committees led in 1957 to a report recommending a unified Single Copy Order Plan. Revised over the years, the plan involves prepayment with the order and the use of multiple-copy standard order forms, supplied to any bookseller through the ABA office, thus securing from most publishers a maximum single copy discount.

Convention programs after World War II featured many sessions to help members learn how to improve their management and merchandising methods. In 1952, convention speakers talked about how to get more income by selling toys and records. Sidney Satenstein, head of American Book-Stratford Press, got the ABA to help publicize a drive to encourage the use of books as business gifts. Other speakers explained ways for the bookseller to do promotion by radio and make use of cooperative ads. Panels in 1953 spotlighted the bookseller's use of direct mail, efficiency in buying and sales procedures, and staff training.

At the 1954 meeting, which drew nearly 900 people to Atlantic City, the ABA presented the first of a new series of awards to publishers for promotion that helped booksellers: point of sale items, statement enclosures, separate mailing pieces, kits of items for a single campaign. The problems peculiar to different kinds of booksellers were recognized by holding separate group meetings of large stores and chains, personal shops, shops in college communities, and department stores.

Similar themes were pursued in the next several years at a dozen regional meetings. The dominant trend was positive, said President Joseph Houlihan of Lexington, Kentucky, at the 1955 convention, and he welcomed this especially because the ABA had been "so often negative."

Through the 1960s, management and merchandising continued to be major themes of national and regional meetings. One management topic, that of staff payrolls, seems to have come up at only one national convention, 1962; at that time, an early bird panel reported that staff salaries were generally abysmal. At other panels that year criticism was leveled also at bookstore promotion. Booksellers do not take advantage of the promotion opportunities offered to them, a speaker said. And at a discussion of "how to survive price-cutting," Igor Kropotkin of the Scribner Bookstore, New York, suggested that booksellers could not expect outside help against price competition: "Our destiny is in our hands alone," he declared.

It was precisely in order to help booksellers strengthen each others' hands that leading booksellers described, at panels and workshop meetings, their own promotion and advertising, their sales and mailings, their specialized departments, their staff training, their handling of inventory. Experts talked on store security.

As a practical demonstration, the ABA introduced in the trade exhibit at the Washington convention in 1962 its own Model Bookstore, exemplifying display and promotional methods, stocked with publishers' current titles, and manned by expert Washington area personnel. From time to time, techniques for recording sales, handling inventory, preventing theft and dealing with other problems were demonstrated. Newcomers to bookselling were especially invited to visit the Model Bookstore for advice and suggestions. This began the ABA's long-standing practice of enlisting a group of experienced members at each convention to make themselves available for consultation with new and prospective booksellers.

"Learning sessions"—informational and how-to meetings—were especially stressed at the 1973 convention, the first full convention in the West in ABA history. Large numbers of booksellers attended who had never been to an annual meeting before. One of the sessions dealt with the "new breed" of booksellers—young, innovative, flexible, educated, consumer-oriented men and women, often unconventional, and in most cases dedicated to bookselling.

Ever since the early 1920s, when an earlier "new breed" was coming to the fore—keepers of "personal bookshops" and a few brilliant specialists in children's books—the ABA had been holding panels on specialized kinds of bookselling and merchandising. Discussions of the children's book field were renewed late in the 1940s. In the 1950s, the Children's Book Council (editors and publishers) had space at the conventions, and in most years since the mid-1960s the CBC took part in convention programs on children's books.

Religious books, similarly, were the topics of specialized sessions from the 1920s onward. For some years, Lenten and other book lists of traditional material were used by ABA members. In recent years, the Religious Publishers' Group cooperated in ABA panels on trends in this increasingly widely defined field. Other specialties have had occasional attention—technical books, rare books—but only once, apparently, has there been a major session on the novel. That was in 1974, and it drew an audience of several hundred.

For many years both mass market and trade paperbacks were puzzling to booksellers—how to order them, where to put them, how to make them pay—and through the 1950s ABA held occasional discussions of them. A particularly important session was led at an Atlanta regional in 1956 by Roysce Smith then of Davison's. He emphasized the bookstore potential of paperbacks in what *PW* called a "seminal" talk on the subject." In 1960, the ABA held its first extensive review of relations with paperback suppliers, and early in 1961 Kroch's & Brentano's prepared and ABA issued the first *Basic Booklist of Paperback Titles* —300 titles in 16 categories. Paperbacks became a feature of the Model Bookshop in 1968.

Since the mid-1920s, ABA has been consistently involved in

the cooperative promotion of reading as well as in promotional services for members. Most booksellers have enthusiastically used the Children's Book Week materials since that celebration began in 1919; have promoted the Newbery and Caldecott children's book award winners; and have taken part in book fairs. Convention panels have explained the pesky problems and successful techniques of operating book fairs and bazaars. In this connection, the ABA in 1952 sent around the country, for exhibit, two sets of 300 juvenile books chosen by the CBC.

In 1949 the ABA joined with the American Book Publishers Council and the Book Manufacturers' Institute to co-sponsor in 1950 the first presentation of the industry's joint National Book Awards (originated in 1948 by the BMI as the Gutenberg Award). In 1954 the nonprofit National Book Committee was formed "to keep books free, make them widely available and encourage people to read." The Committee launched National Library Week (actually a year-round reading promotion effort) in 1958 and was given the administration of the NBA in 1959. Bookstore collaboration in these efforts was uneven, though often effective on a local level. But the committee's nationwide, cumulative impact was significant, even if intangible, for most stores.

In the New York area, the Book-and-Author Luncheons conducted by the New York *Herald Tribune* and ABA jointly, beginning in 1937, were widely popular and, at one time, brought business to the area bookstores that promoted them. The program provided a model, also, for luncheon programs in many other cities. After the *H-T* expired in 1966, the *Book World* review supplement and later *Saturday Review/World* were co-sponsors. But the 1973 season was the last for the New York luncheons. Their function had largely been replaced by TV talk shows. Outside New York City, where community and newspaper involvement were possible, the luncheons continue to thrive.

An ambitious cooperative book advertising and bookstore promotion scheme was tried in 1959 and 1960—four seasonal cooperative ads in regional editions of *Time*, at Christmas and in the spring, with supporting radio and poster promotion, with as many as 26 publishers and 100 booksellers sharing costs, and with bookstore names and locations listed in the ads. Two of these promotions had co-sponsors—Oxford Paper for one, *PW* for another. The results seemed financially favorable for most participants, but the trouble involved discouraged any repetition.

The Changing Convention and Trade Exhibit

Although the ABA, especially after its first dozen years, has always been a center of year-round activity, it is at the annual conventions that its programs come under the spotlight. The trade exhibits have come both to accentuate and almost to dominate the conventions.

The exhibits grew out of the very modest Buyers' Book Browse—a small assemblage of simple displays—held on the last day of the 1947 convention. The next year, this was expanded into a formal trade exhibit, with 117 display areas. Thereafter—except when it was skipped in 1950—the trade show grew each year.

For several years after the show was established, some publishers were not quite sure how to use it and were skeptical about its value. But by the time of the 1954 convention, most had adopted the basic techniques that were employed ever after: specially designed, well-lighted displays, well manned, with emphasis on books of the fall season ahead, promotion materials on hand and, as the years went on, growing numbers of special discount offers and other inducements to early ordering. Admittedly there were always some publishers who saw more trouble than profit in the trade show. Most publishers found the show increasingly necessary for arousing or strengthening interest in their lists; for pulling in early orders; for making possible conversations with booksellers from all parts of the country; for helping the publishers determine first printing orders; and even for deciding on final publication schedules; and for buying and selling subsidiary rights. Today, there is an increasing element of international trading, with booksellers coming from abroad as well as the buying and selling of foreign rights.

As convention attendance climbed, devices to draw attention to individual exhibits or all of them became significant. Raffles, door prizes and souvenirs became commonplace. The visitor to an ABA convention could be easily identified by the well-filled publisher-labelled shopping bags he or she was carrying. By the mid-1960s, authors of forthcoming titles were appearing at many publishers' booths. In the 1970s, eye-catching professional models were hired by some exhibitors, and show business people came to the ABA looking for the news photographers. A portion of the ABA's Model Bookshop was set aside for autographing, and booksellers formed long lines as they waited to have authors sign advance copies of potential best sellers. The ABA has consistently made space available for press conferences for its guest speakers, and in recent years has set up conferences for other current book authors as well. In 1974, nearly a hundred authors attended the convention to meet the press and booksellers and sometimes, each other.

The individual book-and-author publicity at the conventions is considered to have sometimes overshadowed, at least in press reports, the serious work done in book-business discussions and in the buyers' show. Furthermore, it has been easy for the press to spotlight the show business personalities and to forget the distinguished and interesting public figures and serious writers who have graced the ABA sessions from the beginning.

Public figures who have spoken or appeared at the ABA have included the Duke of Windsor, who said he found himself at home among booksellers because he, too, was a salesman—of an empire; Eleanor Roosevelt, who on two different occasions beguiled ABA listeners; Dr. Martin Luther King, Jr., former Presidents Truman and Eisenhower, Adlai Stevenson and many others. Authors—to name a handful among scores—whose talks were remembered for more than a season have ranged from Mark Twain to Kurt Vonnegut. They have included poets of several kinds—Gellett Burgess, Rod McKuen, Phyllis McGinley, Archibald MacLeish, John Ciardi; historians and critics—John Gunther, Arthur Schlesinger, Jr., Margaret Mead, Arnold J. Toynbee, Bernard DeVoto, William L. Shirer; cartoonists—Rube Goldberg, Herblock, Walt Kelly; journalists—Jack Anderson, denouncing abuse of executive power with a preacher's fervor, and Art Buchwald, doing the same with a humorist's hilarious satire; and elegant, deliciously amusing ladies—Emily Kimbrough, Julie Andrews, Ilka Chase.

Along with the serious speakers and topics at the ABA meetings, the conventions have often been occasions for spoofery. One example was a burlesque issue of *PW—Publisher's Weakly, The Heart and Liver of the Booktrade,* circulated in 1931. A different sort of spoof that has lasted, more or less, up to this writing began at the 1961 convention—the Oblivion Press (logo, *O.P.*). The point about it was entirely negative.

Created over the years by a fluid group of sales-advertising people,[5] the Oblivion Press did not exist. It purported to have a sales manager, John Dense, whose slogan was "We take orders from no one." Its first titles included "Main Line Girl—A Philadelphia Heroin," "The Case of the Dead Issue," "Is There Life on Schenectady?" and two juvenile lines including "The Arson Boys' First Flame" (followed in another year by "The Arson Boys Under the Playpen"), "The Egghead Boys Shave with Occam's Razor" and "The Egghead Boys Break Gresham's Law." A title not published in 1966 was "The Complete Book of Power Failures, as told to Connie Edison." O.P. announced an advertising campaign in such former journals as the New York *Sun, Collier's,* the Boston *Transcript* and *St. Nicholas.* Its returns policy was stated as, "Don't Unpack—Just Ship Back."

ABA's International Interests

The convention programs and exhibits were elements, but not the only ones, in the ABA's development of international interests. In 1949, the ABA began administering, in the U.S.A., the UNESCO Book Coupon Plan, which was employed for some years to facilitate international book purchase payments. A few years later, since a number of booksellers were particularly interested in foreign books, Mr. Duffy organized a new (1956) convention feature, an international section of the trade exhibit. This so impressed Frederic G. Melcher of *PW* that he sponsored an expense-paid trip that fall for Mr. Duffy to the Frankfurt International *Book Fair* to explore international bookseller-publisher contacts. In 1960, the ABA arranged a chartered flight of several score booksellers to Frankfurt. While there, Mr. Duffy formally applied for ABA membership in the newly established

[5]Richard E. Bye, Ed Delafield, C.B. Boutell, Fon Boardman, George Wieser, Dick Snyder, Lee Simmons, Paul Eriksson, George Lovitt, Bob Carter, Denny Hatch, and others.

International Community of Booksellers Association. The booksellers were guests of that group and of the British, French, Swiss and German trade associations.

The international exhibits continued as a separate section of the annual trade exhibit until 1968, under the direction of Alexander Wales. After the conventions, the international exhibits were shown during the summer sessions at Columbia University, where on several occasions forums were held on the world book trade.

JUNE 4, 1962

ALVA H. PARRY, PRESIDENT

AMERICAN BOOKSELLERS ASSOCIATION

C/O THE SHOREHAM HOTEL

WASHINGTON, D. C.

AS AN AUTHOR, LOYAL TO THE TRADITIONS OF HIS CRAFT, I AM DEEPLY SORRY NOT TO BE ABLE TO JOIN YOU IN PERSON IN ORDER TO DISCUSS THE INADEQUACY OF THE SALES OF A BOOK CALLED WHY ENGLAND SLEPT. HOWEVER, MY BROTHER, WHOSE BOOK SOLD EVEN LESS WELL THAN MINE, WILL COME AMONG YOU TONIGHT, AND I ADVISE NO ONE TO APPEAR WITHOUT COPIES OF THE ENEMY WITHIN. I TRUST THAT THE ATTORNEY GENERAL'S APPEARANCE WILL INSPIRE YOU ALL TO SELL MORE BOOKS TO MORE PEOPLE THAN EVER BEFORE IN THE NEXT TWELVE MONTHS. NOW THAT READING IS BECOMING INCREASINGLY RESPECTABLE IN AMERICA, I WANT, BOTH AS AN AUTHOR AND AS A READER, TO EXPRESS MY GRATITUDE TO THE MEN AND WOMEN WHO LIVED WITH BOOKS, LOVED THEM, SOLD THEM AND KEPT THEM AN INDISPENSABLE PART OF LIFE. WITH ALL BEST WISHES

JOHN F. KENNEDY

Each international show was opened with a well-publicized International Night, usually with a distinguished speaker. In 1962 the speaker was Attorney General Robert F. Kennedy, who urged strengthening the distribution of U.S. cultural materials "in the uncommitted nations." ABA leaders started acting quickly on this suggestion, issuing a list of basic American books that was sent to 100 countries. Not long after that, the Government Advisory Committee on International Book and Library Programs was formed. It operates with a secretariat under the

Department of State, and comprises 12 members representing publishing, educational and library interests, with the managing directors of the ABA, the AAP and other relevant organizations as official observers. This Committee is now in its 13th year, meeting quarterly in Washington.

The Turmoil of the Times

The conventions have repeatedly reflected the turbulence of the times during ABA's life. As we have seen, the annual meetings were occasions for organizing the book trade for support of national programs in two world wars, and for mobilizing the trade behind the National Recovery Administration during the Depression. In 1968, unlike numerous other industry groups, the ABA was not frightened away from Washington by the race-related disturbances and burnings there. It did not cancel its meetings, suffered little if any loss of attendance and no loss of exhibitors. The 1968 convention was still in session when the shattering news came that Robert Kennedy had been assassinated; and the members were the more deeply affected as they recalled his challenging speech to them six years earlier.

The 1970 convention took place at a moment of heightened anger over the Vietnam War. Display space and discussion time were given to the subject, and some members argued that the ABA should not be lobbying Congress for its own interests— book post rates and educational funds—but for an end to the slaughter in Southeast Asia.

ABA and the Freedom to Read

In its early days the ABA was less concerned about censorship than about insuring the booksellers' reputations for selling "wholesome" rather than "impure" or "improper" or "indecent" literature. The long-standing, extremely comprehensive criminal laws and postal regulations against "lascivious" material were the norms for the respectable bookseller. The ABA apparently took no action in support of any bookseller prosecuted on moral grounds nor of those persecuted in the political raids during the 1919–1921 postwar era.

But as the 1920s went on, censorship for supposed moral reasons caused concern. The 1923 convention discussed the matter and agreed that to publish and exploit "unclean" books was deplorable; but they saw no way to agree on what was "unclean." By 1925, ABA secretary Belle M. Walker took a different tack, supporting the anti-censorship view that "the cure for a flood of unworthy books is borne on its own tide."

At the 1926 convention the ABA's governors offered a statement: "The Board of Trade for the last several years has stated its opposition to federal, state, and municipal censorship of books. . . . The Board of Trade is opposed to the publication and distribution of salacious books. The publishing and sale of books primarily *on the basis* of their salacious appeal invites censorship with its obvious evils. Intelligence, good taste, a sense of humor, and common sense are the board of censorship to whose dictates publishers, booksellers and the reading public should conform."

The problem did not go away, and in 1930, the ABA held, at its eastern convention, its first full-dress panel on censorship. Taking various anti-censorship views were: Mary Ware Dennett, author of "The Sex Side of Life"; H.V. Kaltenborn of the Brooklyn *Eagle,* later a famed radio commentator; Morris L. Ernst, prominent civil liberties lawyer. On the other side was the arch-censor of the era, John S. Sumner, secretary of the New York Society for the Suppression of Vice, who declared with a straight face: "There is no censorship of books."

In the World War II period, censorship was not a notable issue for the ABA, but in the early 1950s there was a crisis. American libraries at home and abroad were forced to remove many books in the hysteria engendered by Sen. Joseph R. McCarthy, who was conducting an ostensibly anti-communist campaign that was, in effect, deeply anti-American in its assault on freedom of inquiry and expression. The ABA passed no resolutions about this, but in 1953 it officially endorsed the *Freedom to Read* declaration issued by librarians and publishers through the National Book Committee. In 1955 Mr. Duffy found himself in a widely broadcast radio debate defending booksellers against a journalist and author, Ralph de Toledano, who claimed that "anti-communist" books were not selling especially well because of "dirty work in the bookstores."

In 1962, ABA convention speakers (authors of new books)—a journalist, Inez Robb, and a famous attorney, Edward Bennett Williams—discussed a new wave of unofficial attacks on The Bill of Rights as it affected books. In 1964, the ABA circulated to members Peter S. Jennison's article, "Censorship: Strategy for Defense," written for the projected *Manual on Bookselling.*

From 1969 into the early 1970s, successive ABA presidents, in their annual reports, defended books and the other media against the attacks then being launched in speeches by Vice President Agnew and other supporters of the Nixon Administration.

Some of these attacks harked back to the U.S. Supreme Court's Roth decision of 1957, which had made possible increasing openness in print, film, and other media, on sexual matters. Then, in June, 1973, the Court issued a highly confusing partial reversal of that decision. ABA leaders became alarmed at the resulting incidents of local and state harassment of booksellers and librarians and at newly introduced state censorship bills. In September the ABA board protested the new ruling and affirmed its agreement with the anti-censorship majority report of the President's Commission on Obscenity and Pornography.

Also in 1973, a group of media people formed, for the first time, a coalition to circulate information on state legislation resulting from the Supreme Court's June decisions and to organize and advise local groups who were concerned about possible adverse laws. Led by Ken McCormick for the AAP, the group included representatives from ABA, the National Association of College Stores, the Motion Picture Association of America, the Council for Periodical Distributors Associations, the International Periodical Distributors Association, the Magazine Publishers Association, and Periodical and Book Association of America. Although they were unable to persuade the broadcast and newspaper segments of the communication industry to join them, they called themselves the Media Coalition, and they are a major national group fighting to uphold the First Amendment against widespread assaults. The ABA's participation marked its first full commitment to anti-censorship efforts.

The next year, meeting in Washington, the ABA held its second major panel on censorship. The legal and practical damage done since the new ruling's issuance was explained by Ken McCormick of Doubleday, Chairman of the Freedom to Read Committee of the Association of American Publishers; Sandy Rector, Pennsylvania bookseller who had become a specialist on censorship problems of bookshops; attorney Barbara Scott, a majority member of the President's Commission; Maxwell J. Lillienstein, ABA counsel. The other speaker, Winfrey C. Link, a minority member of the Commission, surprised his hearers by saying *he* was surprised that "legitimate" booksellers were worried about the threatened new obscenity legislation.

Education for Bookselling

As the need for professionalism in book retailing became more and more obvious, systematic programs—or *a* program—came into being in the mid-1960s. Up to then, training of all kinds had been informal and usually confined to the individual store or organization. Some of the best education was—and still is—undoubtedly provided by attendance at ABA conventions and regional meetings, careful study of trade exhibits, and participation in forums and workshop discussions of bookstore operations and problems.

The ABA has repeatedly emphasized the need for instructional activities, starting, as noted earlier, with courses in New York and Philadelphia in 1913. The 1925 ABA code of ethics recommended that staff training programs be held in a number of cities, and this was followed up the next year in New York and Pittsburgh, as already mentioned.

Systematic bookstore management education can really be said to have begun, with the establishment, by the National Association of College Stores, of a course of several days' duration, called The Booksellers Seminar. In 1969 this program became a joint operation, considerably expanded, of NACS and ABA, under the name, National Booksellers School.

The School is now held twice a year, once in the East and once in the West, with an extremely detailed, five-day, breakfast-to-bedtime curriculum, which is reviewed annually by a faculty committee for refinements. It is taught by leading booksellers who are paid only their expenses, and donate their time. This extraordinary program trains about 300 students per year, from bookstores throughout the country, with scholarships available. Since 1966 the program has turned out some 2000 graduates. This cannot fail to have a long-range, positive impact on the operation of the American book trade.

Instructional literature about bookselling has developed more or less sporadically. ABA members and officers cooperated in several informative pamphlet publications about many aspects of the trade over the past three or four decades.

Several times a week someone comes into the ABA office in New York to ask for advice about opening a bookstore. To help such visitors, the ABA prepared a pamphlet on that topic in 1973, and permanently assigned a staff member to answer questions.

By far the most comprehensive bookselling educational publication has been, of course, *A Manual on Bookselling*, published jointly with R.R. Bowker Co., which handled sales to libraries and other non-members. Many of the articles in its first edition in 1969 appeared originally in an ABA Section which ran in 1964 and 1965 in *PW*, and were reprinted and mailed with the *ABA Bulletin*. The new, 1974 revision edited by Charles B. Anderson, G. Roysce Smith and Sanford Cobb is more comprehensive, and 35 out of its 49 articles are brand new. While ABA continued to distribute a free copy to each of its members, the association thought that bookselling as a career was attracting so much outside interest that the book was offered to a trade publisher, Harmony Books (Crown), which, in keeping with the times, published it in both cloth and paper.

In 1972 the ABA introduced a cassette training program. The first tape was "Tools of the Trade," issued jointly with NACS. The multi-media trend was reaching the ABA.

Forum of the Book Trade

Perhaps no one can mark the precise time when the ABA became an obviously Big Organization. It may have been in 1966, when main-store membership passed 2,000. Perhaps it was when an old hand could go to a trade exhibit and get lost in it.

Certainly it had happened by 1967, when Joe Duffy estimated the full attendance at the annual convention—registered book people plus visitors—at 3500. In 1970 the round number was 4500. In 1971, in Boston (the first move away from the Shoreham Hotel in Washington in 11 years) the change was so refreshing that 5000 people showed up. For 1973, in Los Angeles, the guess was 7000, and in 1974, at the Sheraton-Park in Washington, the ABA office reported "over 7000" attending, with 520 spaces occupied by 332 exhibitors, including 50 who were new to the trade show.

Bookstores obviously were not dying off, as the Chicago *Tribune* had recklessly suggested a few years earlier. Joe Duffy and the ABA board had built up the trade exhibit, invited both experts and celebrities to speak, and encouraged publishers to bring authors and show them off. Programs were built around members' replies to a questionnaire on what they wanted discussed.

Before the 1972 convention, Robert L. Hale of Hathaway House, Wellesley, Mass., had written in *PW* that booksellers should attend the convention because it is "a marketplace, an *agora* where books are bought and sold and information is exchanged." The panels, he advised, are occasions for picking up ideas if one goes in "with a receptive attitude." The "boisterous" publisher-bookseller relations (or "gripe") sessions constitute a valuable forum, he said. That point was underlined by a speaker at one of the gripe sessions, who called it a "constructively relentless" exchange of criticism and suggestions.

Joseph Duffy succumbed to a heart attack on the last afternoon of the 1972 meeting. The banquet that night could not be cancelled; it was held, and leaders spoke briefly and warmly in tribute to Mr. Duffy's memory.

He had died not at the end of an era; instead he had presided over the beginning of a new one. G. Roysce Smith, who had joined the ABA staff from the Yale Co-op in 1971 to be educational director, was appointed later in 1972 to succeed Mr. Duffy.

The ABA was already working on ways to cope with the inescapable problems of growth—greater numbers of books and booksellers, new demands upon the association, an increasingly complex book industry and increasingly varied markets. The

1974 convention pointed to one of the directions of the future when it featured a discussion for members interested in regional associations; a Big Organization must be hospitable to smaller, congenial units. The ABA's educational and publications projects have begun to point to other tasks which the association knows it must undertake.

It has been evident to ABA leaders for a long time that effective bookselling to the general and specialized book audiences requires well-educated booksellers. Bookselling therefore must be not only spiritually but economically attractive to educated people. Knowing this, the ABA can be expected to focus increased efforts upon making bookselling feasible for people who truly care about books and their importance; who see themselves indeed as good merchants—but, being booksellers, as much more than merchants.

I V

Best Sellers in the Bookstores
1900-1975

by Alice Payne Hackett,

author of *50 Years of Best Sellers, 60 Years of Best
Sellers, 70 Years of Best Sellers,* and the forthcoming
80 Years of Best Sellers.

We shall not busy ourselves with what men ought to have admired, what they ought to have written, what they ought to have thought, but what they did think, write, admire.

GEORGE SAINTSBURY, *A History of Criticism*

The Early Years

It's a long way from *To Have and to Hold* by Mary Johnston in 1900 to the current best sellers. Today's booksellers may scarcely recognize the titles and authors at the top of the early best seller lists. Essentially all these lists were compiled in the same way, from reports by booksellers. They were and still are based on trade sales exclusive of book club, direct mail or non-store outlets, and therefore are most pertinent to this volume. It is my purpose in this article, as well as mentioning some of the characteristic best sellers from 1900 to the present, to indicate how they indeed reflect changing mores and historical events.

The early years of this century were dominated by the historical novel. Winston Churchill's latest work appeared first on best seller lists nearly every other year. (He was, of course, the American not the British Winston Churchill.) Many of the best sellers of these early years sold more than 100,000 or even

200,000 copies. There were no paperback reprints nor any book clubs, and the originals remained in print much longer. It was at this time too, that American authors began to figure prominently on the annual lists. 1906 saw the first all-American best seller list. Previously British novelists had dominated, some of whom, like Arthur Conan Doyle and Rudyard Kipling, are better known to today's readers than their American counterparts. Exceptions were Booth Tarkington, who first appeared on the list in 1902, and Edith Wharton, whose *The House of Mirth* became a best seller in 1905. By this year both business as a theme and the inventions of the early twentieth century were reflected in serious as well as light fiction. Most of the publicity pictures of authors showed them at the wheels of their new automobiles.

In 1909, Mary Roberts Rinehart was the first American author to make the best seller list with a straight detective story, *The Man in Lower Ten.* The detective or suspense story has remained popular and sometimes dominates annual fiction lists, although often in greatly altered form and substance. The simple whodunits (except in the case of Agatha Christie) have been replaced by the spy story, in which the suspense derives from real-life situations, and even by thrillers about national and international business and politics, again reflecting or even predicting the events of our changing world.

In 1910 the biggest best seller was *The Rosary* by Florence Barclay. So profitable was this book that its publisher, G.P. Putnam, erected a building on 45th Street in New York just west of Fifth Avenue, which in the trade was nicknamed "The Rosary Building." Mary Roberts Rinehart, then published by Bobbs-Merrill, had two novels, not essentially whodunits, on the 1910 list. A best-selling author for more than 50 years, she produced her first and most popular straight romantic novel, *K,* in 1915. Her last hardcover best seller was *The Doctor* in 1936, published by Farrar & Rinehart. Her biggest seller in hardcover has been a whodunit, *The Circular Staircase.*

The New York Public Library at 42nd Street and Fifth Avenue was opened in 1911, a year which marked the emergence among the top ten of Harold Bell Wright and Gene Stratton Porter, many of whose books became all-time best sellers. Most sales of these two authors were augmented by their republication in hardcover reprints at 50 or 75 cents, usually by Grosset & Dunlap or A.L. Burt & Co. Topping the 1911 list was *The Broad Highway* by the new British author Jeffrey Farnol; it seemed to mark the peak of an era of popularity for the romantic historical novel.

Prior to 1912 booksellers had reported only fifteen best sellers, because until then nonfiction sales did not warrant their inclusion on the lists. Times have changed. Now it is quite usual for annual nonfiction sales to outnumber fiction sales by two to one, especially when there are numerous "how to's" (ranging from philosophy and psychology to sex) available. In 1912 and 1913 *Publishers Weekly* added a nonfiction list, then dropped it for three years. In 1917 and 1918, there were three categories of best sellers: fiction, general nonfiction, and war books. By 1919, after World War I, the fiction and nonfiction lists were set up as we know them today.

Gene Stratton Porter's *The Harvester* headed the fiction of rather poor quality in 1912. But in this first year that nonfiction was included, there was an impressive list of books and authors headed by *The Promised Land* by Mary Antin, and followed by volumes by Madame Montessori, James Bryce, Jane Addams, Eugène Brieux, Arnold Bennett, Henri Bergson, and Olive Schreiner.

The Twenties

Lightweight fiction continued to dominate fiction lists until 1921, with such remembered books as *Penrod* and *Seventeen* by Booth Tarkington; *Mr. Britling Sees It Through*, a war novel by H.G. Wells, which sold 350,000 copies in 15 months; *The Four Horsemen of the Apocalypse* by V. Blasco Ibañez (with a new high price for fiction, $1.90); and *The Arrow of Gold* by Joseph Conrad.

The renaissance in American creative writing was reflected to some extent by bookstore best sellers in 1921 when Sinclair Lewis's *Main Street* sold 295,000 copies. This new realism was to replace the romantic novel of previous years. Dorothy Canfield's *The Brimming Cup* was second on the 1921 list, both books published by the new firm of Harcourt, Brace & Co., and Edith Wharton's *The Age of Innocence* was fourth. Markedly different was Edith M. Hull's *The Sheik*, which might be considered the forerunner of the sex novel. As the basis of a movie it brought Rudolph Valentino to fame. The next best-selling novel of this new daring appeared in 1925, *The Green Hat* by Michael Arlen, and then Viña Delmar's *Bad Girl* made the lists in 1928. The Roaring Twenties were represented later by Katherine Brush's *Young Man of Manhattan*. Two of the most significant books about the younger generation of the twenties and thirties never made the top ten, Fitzgerald's novel, *This Side of Paradise*, and Warner Fabian's *Flaming Youth*.

Sinclair Lewis was a best-selling author for many years, one novel after another: in 1922 and 1923, *Babbitt; Arrowsmith* in 1925; *Elmer Gantry*, which took top place in 1927 with sales of more than 200,000 in its first ten weeks; *Dodsworth*, which was second in 1929; *Ann Vickers* in 1933; *It Can't Happen Here*, a prophetic story of World War II, in 1937; *Cass Timberlane* in 1945; and *Kingsblood Royal*, in which he dealt with racism, in 1947.

Although traditional works of both American and British authors prevailed in the twenties and thirties, writers of greater literary quality emerged. There were Edna Ferber, Margaret Kennedy, E. Barrington, John Erskine and John Galsworthy, whose first best seller, *The Silver Spoon*, appeared in 1926, and whose *Forsyte Saga* is well known to modern book buyers, especially since its great success on public television. Also new to the lists were Louis Bromfield with *A Good Woman* in 1927, and Thornton Wilder, whose *The Bridge of San Luis Rey* was a remarkable hit of 1928, selling 240,000 in its first year. Following closely was *Wintersmoon*, Hugh Walpole's first best seller in this country.

The Thirties and Forties

In 1929, the first novelist other than British or American to make his appearance on these fiction lists was the German-born Erich Maria Remarque with *All Quiet on the Western Front*, the best-known novel about World War I. The next year J.B. Priestley made his first big hit in this country with *Angel Pavement*. In 1931, half the best-selling novels were by women, all American but one. The leader was Pearl S. Buck with *The Good Earth*, repeating her achievement with the same book the next year. On the same list was *Grand Hotel* by Vicki Baum, originator of a type of plot that is still in use. 1932 saw the first appearance of Lloyd C. Douglas, unostentatiously in eighth place. His *Magnificent Obsession* was one of those rare books that build up a quiet following achieved by word of mouth rather than by publishers' publicity and advertising. With this first book, Douglas, a retired minister, began a best-selling career and in 1943 launched a revival of the religious and historical religious novel, when his *The Robe* headed the fiction best seller list. *Green Light* in 1935, and *The Big Fisherman* both added to his position as a best-selling author. In the years between other religious and semi-religious historical novels headed the lists: *The Keys of the Kingdom* by A.J. Cronin in 1941; Franz Werfel's *The Song of Bernadette* in 1942, which with its clothbound reprint edition sold more than 900,000 copies in two years; *The Miracle of the Bells* by Russell Janney in 1947; *The Egyptian* by Mika Waltari in 1949; *The Cardinal* by Henry Morton Robinson in 1950; and *The Silver Chalice* by Thomas B. Costain in 1952. Among historical novels, the memorable *Anthony Adverse* by Hervey Allen reigned for two years, 1933 and 1934. Perhaps best-known to today's readers, aided by its movie revival and a new paperback edition, was *Gone With the Wind* by Margaret Mitchell, top seller in 1936 and 1937. The then notorious *Forever Amber* by Kathleen Winsor was first in 1945, and *The King's General* by Daphne DuMaurier headed the list in 1946. *The King's General* sold 228,000 copies through the trade, but three book clubs brought sales up to more than a million. The second title on that 1946 list, Taylor Caldwell's *This Side of Innocence,* had a good bookstore sale of 221,000, but the largest sale ever attained until then by a Literary Guild selection brought sales to more than 1,055,000 copies.

Fiction leaders in these years were by such writers of the new era as John Steinbeck with *The Grapes of Wrath,* which sold 300,000 bookstore copies; Richard Llewellyn with *How Green Was My Valley; Strange Fruit* by Lillian Smith; and *From Here to Eternity* by James Jones, a novel about U.S. Army men which culminated in the attack on Pearl Harbor.

Not to be overlooked among the best-selling fiction of this period are James Hilton's *Good-bye, Mr. Chips,* the first book to become famous through radio recommendation when it was praised by Alexander Woolcott. Thomas Wolfe, whose first novel, *Look Homeward Angel,* had been a literary success, first reached the best-seller audience in 1935, with his second book, *Of Time and the River.* Notable for literary quality on the 1936 list were *The Last Puritan* by George Santayana, *The Thinking Reed* by Rebecca West, and *Eyeless in Gaza* by Aldous Huxley. Walter Edmonds, with *Drums Along the Mohawk,* was a neophyte in this period of historical fiction, as was Kenneth Roberts with *North-west Passage* in 1937. By 1947 when half the fiction list was made up of historical novels, Roberts' biggest success, *Lydia Bailey,* was in fourth place. In addition to *Northwest Passage,* 1937 intro-duced *The Years* by Virginia Woolf, *Theatre* by W. Somerset Maugham, and *Of Mice and Men* by John Steinbeck. A significant new type of novel appeared in 1938, the forerunner of one of today's most popular types, both in hardcover and paperback, the Gothic. This was Daphne Du Maurier's *Rebecca.* John P. Marquand, whose popularity was to continue for many years, first became a best seller in 1939 with *Wickford Point,* although his *The Late George Apley* in 1937 had brought him to the attention of readers, booksellers, and critics.

The beginning of World War II in Europe was reflected in such best-selling novels as *Escape* by Ethel Vance in 1939 and *Mrs. Miniver* by Jan Struther in 1940. Ernest Hemingway, originator of a great new style of writing, appeared on the 1940 list with his novel of the Spanish Civil War, *For Whom the Bell Tolls.* Continuing the vogue for historical novels was F. van Wyck Mason's *Stars on the Sea.* Surprisingly World War II was seldom the subject of best-selling novels during the war years. In 1943 there were only two wartime books among the top ten, *So Little Time* by John P. Marquand and *The Human Comedy* by William Saroyan. Again in 1944 there were but two: *The Razor's Edge* by W. Somerset Maugham and John Hersey's first novel, *A Bell for Adano.* In 1945 there were none. Historical fiction predominated, with Kathleen Winsor's *Forever Amber* selling over 850,000 copies in its second year, without benefit of book club distribution.

Bookstore sales were high 30 years ago since books stayed longer in the public eye before the advent of paperbacks and television. Historical novels kept on their course, one significant event being the advent of the black writer, Frank Yerby, with

The Foxes of Harrow. He was to become one of the biggest-selling novelists of the forties and fifties. Another perennially popular novelist, Frances Parkinson Keyes, reached third place with *The River Road* which sold 225,000 in bookstores, combining with book club sales for a total of 950,000 copies. Taylor Caldwell's long best-selling career began at this time with *This Side of Innocence.* Irving Stone, emerging as a best seller with one of his many biographical novels, *Immortal Wife,* reached his peak in 1961 with *The Agony and the Ecstasy,* based on the life of Michelangelo.

Social problems became the theme of many best sellers, among them such books as *Earth and High Heaven* by Gwethalyn Graham in 1945, and in 1946 both *The Hucksters* by Frederic Wakeman, which satirized the advertising business, and *The Snake Pit* by Mary Jane Ward, which depicted psychiatric problems. One of the most popular books of this time was *Gentlemen's Agreement* by Laura Z. Hobson, which had to do with anti-Semitism.

There were two World War II novels on the 1948 list, *The Naked and the Dead* by Norman Mailer, and *The Young Lions* by Irwin Shaw. Another first novelist, Ross Lockridge, Jr., whose *Raintree County* was perhaps most widely praised of all by critics, was among the top ten in 1948. Coincidentally, as this is being written, Lockridge is one subject of a dual portrait by John Leggett, *Ross and Tom,* reviewed on the front page of the *New York Times Book Review.* The Tom is Thomas Higgen, whose *Mister Roberts* was published in 1946. Both men were suicides.

Another new author, John O'Hara, cropped up on the 1949 list with *A Rage to Live* which reached fourth place and sold 135,000 copies. His first and perhaps his best book, *Appointment in Samarra,* had not made the lists when it was published a few years earlier. It became the custom for O'Hara's publisher, Random House, to issue his new novels or books of short stories on Thanksgiving Day each year.

The Fifties

Most of the novelists on the best seller lists in the 1950's are well known to booksellers today. No very noticeable trends were in evidence, until the beginning of the era of permissiveness in the arts, with the sex novel. The first glimpse at a possible future came with *Peyton Place* by Grace Metalious, one of the big best sellers of all time, today not considered too shocking for TV, where the series is still shown in the most unprime time.

First appearances of modern authors in the fifties were those of Budd Schulberg with *The Disenchanted,* a roman-a-clef about F. Scott Fitzgerald; Herman Wouk in 1951 with *The Caine Mutiny,* a wartime novel of the Navy; James Michener with *Return to Paradise,* a follow-up of his *Tales of the South Pacific,* on which the famous musical, *South Pacific* was based. In 1953, there were five historical novels on the list, and two new authors came to the fore who were destined to continue on their best-selling ways: Ernest K. Gann with *The High and the Mighty,* and Leon M. Uris with *Battle Cry.*

It was during this time that paperbacks began to sell in very large quantities, eroding somewhat the big sales of hardbound novels. There had been reprints in hardcover before this, often movie editions, which outsold the originals. In 1953 *From Here to Eternity* sold 2,000,000 copies in its 75 cent paperback edition, timed to the appearance of the film. And people were just beginning to learn to say, "I'll wait for the paperback."

By 1955, hardbound fiction sales had dropped a bit from the peak of ten years before. *Marjorie Morningstar* by Herman Wouk sold just under 200,000 copies; Patrick Dennis's *Auntie Mame* was second with 150,000; and Simone de Beauvoir was a best seller in 1956 with *The Mandarins.* Another woman writer, Kay Thompson, introduced *Eloise,* child terror of the Plaza Hotel, with illustrations by Hilary Knight, one of the few illustrated fiction best sellers since the early years of the century. Notable at the top of 1957's list was James Gould Cozzens' *By Love Possessed.* Although Cozzens had won the Pulitzer Prize in 1948 with *Guard of Honor,* *By Love Possessed* was his first best seller. Also prominent were *Compulsion* by Meyer Levin, *On the Beach,* a terrifying novel of the nuclear age by Nevil Shute, and *Atlas Shrugged* by Ayn Rand.

Boris Pasternak and Vladimir Nabokov were the first Russian writers to appear on American best seller lists. In 1958 Pasternak's *Doctor Zhivago* led with a big sale of nearly half a million, plus book club copies. In second place was *Anatomy of a Murder* by Robert Traver, a mystery story, by now a rarity among the first 10. Third was the Nabokov novel, *Lolita*, which had a sale of 153,000. Later, because of its popularity as a much less serious film it sold more than three million in paperback. This was also the year of Jerome Weidman's first appearance with a best seller about a Jewish-Gentile marriage, *The Enemy Camp*. D. H. Lawrence, a long-established writer, saw the veil of censorship rent a bit in 1959 to allow the famous *Lady Chatterley's Lover* to be published in this country in unexpurgated form, and it sold about 160,000 copies in that year. During that same time Allen Drury had his first best seller, *Advise and Consent*, one of his many novels based upon political situations. Also significant, in sixth place, was *The Ugly American* by William J. Lederer and Eugene I. Burdick, which concerned American diplomatic behavior in a small southeast Asian country. The modern world was decidedly replacing history as the basis for best-selling novels. At the top of the list in 1959 was Leon Uris's famous *Exodus*, a story of the making of the state of Israel, reaching about 400,000 sales in hardcover. James Michener's long novel, *Hawaii*, in third place, was published as the Islands became our fiftieth state.

The Sixties

In 1960 only two new authors made the list of ten best sellers in fiction: Giuseppe di Lampedusa with a translation from the Italian, *The Leopard*, and Irving Wallace with *The Chapman Report*, another of those which are often referred to as sex novels. *Advise and Consent* and *Hawaii*, both of which had been published in 1959, were number one and two, respectively, in 1960. Irving Stone's *The Agony and the Ecstasy* headed the list in 1961, and second place was claimed by J. D. Salinger's *Franny and Zooey*. This was Salinger's first best seller, for *The Catcher in the Rye* had fallen short of the top ten when it was published in 1951. Other leaders in 1961 were Harper Lee's *To Kill a Mockingbird* and Henry Miller's *Tropic of Cancer*, which sold 100,000 in hardcover and two and a half million in paperback. The surprise best seller of 1961, however, was *Winnie Ille Pu,* a translation into Latin of A. A. Milne's children's classic, *Winnie the Pooh.*

Katherine Anne Porter's *Ship of Fools* led the list in 1962. *Fail-Safe* by Eugene Burdick and *Seven Days in May* by Fletcher Knebel and Charles W. Bailey II were also among the top ten. In 1963 Morris L. West's *The Shoes of the Fisherman* was number one with a rather disappointing bookstore sale of only 170,000 copies, and Mary McCarthy's *The Group* was number two with 130,000. The modern suspense novel came into its own in 1964 when a thriller for the first time outsold all other fiction. This was John Le Carre's *The Spy Who Came in From the Cold,* which had a sale of 230,000 copies in the stores, and a paperback sale the following year of more than two million. Two other suspense novels were on the same list: *You Only Live Twice* by Ian Fleming and *This Rough Magic* by Mary Stewart, both of whom appeared among the top ten for the first time.

The average price of books in the stores had risen in 1965 to $7.65, as compared to $5.29 in 1957–59. Suspense novels continued to be popular, with John Le Carre's *The Looking Glass War* and Ian Fleming's *The Man with the Golden Gun* among the first ten, though Michener's *The Source* easily dominated fiction sales. The year following, Jacqueline Susann's *Valley of the Dolls,* which the *Guinness Book of World Records* cites as the best selling novel of all times, was in first place with sales of over 275,000 copies. Second in 1966 was Harold Robbins' *The Adventurers,* which sold 187,000 copies. Other novelists on the same list were Robert Crichton, Helen MacInnes and Bernard Malamud. 1967 saw Elia Kazan's *The Arrangement* first with sales of 200,000 in the stores, and in 1968 Arthur Hailey's *Airport* was easily the most popular book of the year, having sales of more than a quarter million in the stores. And John Updike and Gore Vidal made the list for the first time.

Reversing trends of the fifties and early sixties, the sales of the top ten novels in 1969 almost equalled those of the top ten in non-fiction. Fiction leader in 1969 was Philip Roth's *Portnoy's Complaint* which had an impressive bookstore sale of 418,000 copies. In second position was *The Godfather* by Mario Puzo, which had sales of 350,000, with later sales in paperback making it one of the all-time best sellers.

The best sellers in fiction from 1970 to 1974 are quite familiar to booksellers. At the top of the list for 1973 and 1974 and another of the best sellers of all time was Richard Bach's *Jonathan Livingston Seagull,* the first novel to keep the lead for two successive years since *Gone With the Wind* in 1936 and 1937. Mystery and suspense have been in great demand by book buyers during the past several years. John Le Carre added to his best-selling record in 1974 with a story generally considered to be his best, *Tinker, Tailor, Soldier, Spy. Love Story* by Erich Segal in 1970 and *Wheels* by Arthur Hailey in 1971 were number one in those years.

Non-fiction in the Twenties and Thirties

As mentioned earlier in this survey, non-fiction was not a regular and separate section of the best seller list in *Publishers Weekly* until 1919. From that year until the present the most popular non-fiction books have run more or less according to a pattern. Dominating the lists have been "how-to" and self-help books, new versions of the Bible, new cookbooks, new dictionaries, books of entertainment, books on the most-discussed issues of the period, and memoirs of presidents, ambassadors, and other men and women of renown. Among the books most in demand through the twenties and thirties were those by H. G. Wells (*Outline of History*); Hendrik Willem Van Loon (*The Story of Mankind, Van Loon's Geography,* and *The Arts*); Lytton Strachey (*Queen Victoria* and *Elizabeth and Essex*); Will Durant (*The Story of Philosophy*); Emil Ludwig (*Napoleon, Lincoln* and *Goethe*); John Gunther (*Inside Europe,* the first of several "Inside" best sellers); and Anne Morrow Lindbergh (*North to the Orient* and *Listen! the Wind*). Though it may be easily argued that much of the non-fiction written in this period was superior in literary quality to most of the fiction, the best-selling novels almost always outsold the non-fiction.

Among the self-help and how-to books of this period *Diet and Health* by Lulu Hunt Peters was a best seller for three consecutive years, 1922, '23, '24. Emily Post's *Etiquette* made its first appearance in print in 1923 and quickly dominated all non-fiction sales. In the same year, Emile Coué made the annual list with *Self Mastery Through Conscious Auto-Suggestion,* the book which told Americans that day by day in every way they were getting better. In 1933 Walter B. Pitkin's *Life Begins at Forty* was number one, number two the year following, and became one of the all-time best sellers, fiction or non-fiction. The next big best seller in the self-help department was Joshua Loth Liebman's *Peace of Mind,* which in 1946 and 1947 sold more than half a million copies. Dr. Liebman was to be surpassed a few years later by Norman Vincent Peale, whose *Power of Positive Thinking* sold well over a million copies between the years of 1952 and 1955. Throughout the years various new editions of the Bible and revised editions of standard cookbooks have sold in great quantities. *The Better Homes and Gardens Cook Book* is the all-time best selling cookbook. With the exception of the Bible, the top-selling title, fiction or non-fiction, in the past 75 years, is Dr. Spock's *Common Sense Book of Baby and Child Care,* which was first published in 1946 and since then has sold more than 2,500,000 copies in cloth and paperback.

Now and then books of poetry and plays are best sellers. Eugene O'Neill's *Strange Interlude* ·(1928), Stephen Vincent Benét's *John Brown's Body* (1929), Edna St. Vincent Millay's *Fatal Interview* (1931), and Alice Duer Miller's *The White Cliffs* (1941) were all among the top sellers in the years of their publication. In more recent times only Rod McKuen among verse writers was a yearly best seller. On the 1968 list there were three of his books, which sold a total of more than 800,000. Kahlil Gibran's *The Prophet* has never been on an annual best seller list since it was first published in 1923, but its sales every year have been impressive. In 1968 alone 373,000 copies of *The Prophet* were sold.

Books of entertainment have been in demand from the twenties onward. The earliest books in this category were the crossword puzzle books published first in 1925 by the newly formed publishing house of Simon and Schuster. Later on in the twenties there was active demand for such books as the Culbertson books on bridge, the Ask Me Another books, and Ripley's Believe It or Not.

Customer demand for books on sex may be said to have originated with the publication in 1948 of the Kinsey Report, *Sexual Behavior in the Human Male,* which was sold at short discount to the stores but which nevertheless had sales of 225,000. In 1953 *Sexual Behavior in the Human Female,* also at short discount, sold 275,000 in the stores. In the 1960's *Sex and the Single Girl* by Helen Gurley Brown and *Human Sexual Response* by Masters and Johnson were solid best sellers. In 1970 two books on sex became really big sellers: Dr. David Reuben's book, *Everything You Always Wanted to Know about Sex but Were Afraid to Ask,* was number one that year with sales of more than 900,000 copies; *The Sensuous Woman* by "J" sold more than 600,000. The following year *The Sensuous Man* by "M" was number one in non-fiction, yet it had sales of only 380,000. In 1973 Dr. Comfort's *The Joy of Sex* had sold 600,000 copies, though it reached only third place on the list behind *The Living Bible* and *I'm O.K., You're O.K.*

The Bible in one form or another is a perennial best seller. In 1972 and 1973 *The Living Bible,* retold by Kenneth Taylor, was far and away the top seller with total sales of well over 3,000,000 copies. Its sales potential was augmented by an arrangement by which Doubleday distributed the book to the trade and Tyndale House sold it to stores such as J. C. Penney which are ordinarily not covered by book travelers. Other new versions of the Bible selling more than a million copies were *The Revised Standard Version,* published by Nelson in 1952, and *The New English Bible,* published jointly by Cambridge and Oxford first in 1962 as the *New Testament* and then in 1970 both Old and New Testaments. There is no historical record of how many copies of the Bible in all its forms and editions have been sold in the last 75 years, but there is no doubt that it has outsold all other books.

Paperbacks

Publishers Weekly began to compile annual lists of paperback best sellers in 1957. For several years, as with the hardback lists, the *PW* editors asked the stores to report their best-selling titles in fiction and non-fiction. Later they compiled separate lists of mass market and quality or trade paperbacks and disregarded the categories of fiction and non-fiction. From 1968 to the present time they have felt themselves on firmer ground by using print orders or publisher's "in print" figures instead of bookseller reports as the basis of their compilation. In the mass market lists, the best-selling titles in paper have nearly always been those books that have already been best sellers in cloth. Joseph Heller's *Catch 22*, which rather surprisingly had not been an annual best seller in hardback, was an exception when it was the top paperback in 1962. On the other hand, in the trade paperback field, the top sellers, with only one exception, *The New English Bible,* had never been best sellers when they were first published in cloth.

Among the all-time best sellers in paperback were the Peanuts books of Charles Schulz. By 1965 Fawcett had 22,000,000 in print with the tide still swelling. In the trade paperback editions of Holt, Rinehart & Winston, the same Peanuts titles were top sellers in their more expensive format. It was in 1965 also that Tolkien's *The Hobbit* and *The Fellowship of the Ring* made the list for the first time. The year following, the earlier two were joined on the list by *The Middle Earth.* At the same time the books of Ian Fleming were in great demand with more than 16 million copies of twelve titles in print in one year.

Toward the end of the decade the movies were becoming a more and more important factor in creating demand for titles in paperback, and a high percentage of the books on the lists were there largely because of their success as films. Books by and about blacks were in increasing demand in paperback, as black was becoming "more beautiful than ever." Science fiction was on the increase, as were books on sports, especially pro football. *Instant Replay* by Jerry Kramer and Dick Schaap had sales in 1969 of more than 2 3/4 million copies.

The paperback market in the 1970's continued to expand and flourish. There was growing demand for gothics, westerns, mysteries, and science fiction. The schools and colleges made increasing use in the classroom of paperbacks of all kinds. Publishers ventured into new fields such as ecology and inspiration. In 1971 the book phenomenon of the year was *The Whole Earth Catalogue* which carried a price tag of $5.00 and sold over 700,000 copies. The top best seller for both 1970 and 1971, however, was Erich Segal's *Love Story,* aided and abetted by the movie. In 1970 alone there were more than 7,000,000 copies of *Love Story* in print.

It was becoming more and more common for paperback publishers to buy the rights to publish a book in both hardback and paper, and then sell the hardback rights to a hardback house. A few attempts were made by paperback companies to publish titles simultaneously in both hardback and paper, the most notable being the publication of Richard Brautigan's *The Abortion*, which had sales in paper of 170,000 and in hardcover of 6,500. Publishers were paying higher sums for paperback rights. Avon, for example, paid more than a million dollars each for *Jonathan Livingston Seagull* and *I'm O.K., You're O.K.* Their faith in both books was rewarded when in 1973 *Seagull* was number one with sales of 6,500,000 copies and *O.K.* was second with 3,800,000. In the 1970's paperback houses expanded into the field of children's books with gratifying results. E. B. White's *Charlotte's Web* was the first to sell a million copies.

Paperback books are sold in more than 100,000 outlets in the United States. With the increasing availability and variety of titles, the future for the paperback would seem to be secure. In the *Saturday Review/World* for August 24, 1974, Norman Podharetz, editor of *Commentary*, takes issue with the statement, sometimes made, that literature may have no future at all. He writes: "Not so many years ago, books were hard to find in the United States; today they are hard to escape. There is no town so small nor hamlet so remote that it does not offer an astonishing number and variety of books for sale at relatively reasonable prices. In what sense such a situation can be interpreted as a portent of the obsolescence of print baffles the mind."

Best Sellers in the Bookstores 1900–1974

Compiled by Alice Payne Hackett

FICTION

1900

To Have and To Hold, by Mary Johnston. Houghton Mifflin
Red Pottage, by Mary Cholmondeley. Harper

1901

The Crisis, by Winston Churchill. Macmillan
Alice of Old Vincennes, by Maurice Thompson. Bowen-Merrill

1902

The Virginians, by Owen Wister. Macmillan
Mrs. Wiggs of the Cabbage Patch, by Alice Caldwell Hegan. Century

1903

Lady Rose's Daughter, by Mrs. Humphry Ward. Harper
Gordon Keith, by Thomas Nelson Page. Scribner

1904

The Crossing, by Winston Churchill. Macmillan
The Deliverance, by Ellen Glasgow. Doubleday, Page

1905

The Marriage of William Ashe, by Mrs. Humphry Ward. Harper
Sandy, by Alice Hegan Rice. Century

1906

Coniston, by Winston Churchill. Macmillan
Lady Baltimore, by Owen Wister. Macmillan

1907

The Lady of the Decoration, by Frances Little. Century
The Weavers, by Gilbert Parker. Harper

1908

Mr. Crewe's Career, by Winston Churchill. Macmillan
The Barrier, by Rex Beach. Harper

1909

The Inner Shrine, Anonymous (Basil King). Harper
Katrine, by Eleanor Macartney Lane. Harper

1910

The Rosary, by Florence Barclay. Putnam
A Modern Chronicle, by Winston Churchill. Macmillan

1911

The Broad Highway, by Jeffrey Farnol. Little, Brown
The Prodigal Judge, by Vaughan Kester. Bobbs-Merrill

1912

The Harvester, by Gene Stratton Porter. Doubleday, Page
The Street Called Straight, by Basil King. Harper

1913

The Inside of the Cup, by Winston Churchill. Macmillan
V. V.'s Eyes, by Henry Sydnor Harrison. Houghton Mifflin

1914

The Eyes of the World, by Harold Bell Wright. Book Supply Co.
Pollyanna, by Eleanor H. Porter. Page

1915

The Turmoil, by Booth Tarkington. Harper
A Far Country, by Winston Churchill. Macmillan

1916

Seventeen, by Booth Tarkington. Harper
When a Man's a Man, by Harold Bell Wright. Book Supply Co.

1917

Mr. Britling Sees It Through, by H. G. Wells. Macmillan
The Light in the Clearing, by Irving Bacheller. Bobbs-Merrill

1918

The U. P. Trail, by Zane Grey. Harper
The Tree of Heaven, by May Sinclair. Macmillan

1919

The Four Horsemen of the Apocalypse, by V. Blasco Ibañez. Dutton
The Arrow of Gold, by Joseph Conrad. Doubleday, Page

1920

The Man of the Forest, by Zane Grey. Harper
Kindred of the Dust, by Peter B. Kyne. Cosmopolitan Book Co.

1921

Main Street, by Sinclair Lewis. Harcourt, Brace
The Brimming Cup, by Dorothy Canfield. Harcourt, Brace

1922

If Winter Comes, by A. S. M. Hutchinson. Little, Brown
The Sheik, by Edith M. Hull. Small, Maynard

1923

Black Oxen, by Gertrude Atherton. Boni & Liveright
His Children's Children, by Arthur Train. Scribner

1924

So Big, by Edna Ferber. Doubleday, Page
The Plastic Age, by Percy Marks. Century

1925

Soundings, by A. Hamilton Gibbs. Little, Brown
The Constant Nymph, by Margaret Kennedy. Doubleday, Page

1926

The Private Life of Helen of Troy, by John Erskine. Bobbs-Merrill
Gentlemen Prefer Blondes, by Anita Loos. Boni & Liveright

1927

Elmer Gantry, by Sinclair Lewis. Harcourt, Brace
The Plutocrat, by Booth Tarkington. Doubleday, Page

1928

The Bridge of San Luis Rey, by Thornton Wilder. A. & C. Boni
Wintersmoon, by Hugh Walpole. Doubleday, Doran

1929

All Quiet on the Western Front, by Erich Maria Remarque. Little, Brown
Dodsworth, by Sinclair Lewis. Harcourt, Brace

1930

Cimarron, by Edna Ferber. Doubleday, Doran
Exile, by Warwick Deeping. Knopf

1931

The Good Earth, by Pearl S. Buck. John Day
Shadows on the Rock, by Willa Cather. Knopf

1932

The Good Earth, by Pearl S. Buck. John Day
The Fountain, by Charles Morgan. Knopf

1933

Anthony Adverse, by Hervey Allen. Farrar & Rinehart
As the Earth Turns, by Gladys Hasty Carroll. Macmillan

1934

Anthony Adverse, by Hervey Allen. Farrar & Rinehart
Lamb in His Bosom, by Caroline Miller. Harper

1935

Green Light, by Lloyd C. Douglas. Houghton Mifflin
Vein of Iron, by Ellen Glasgow. Harcourt, Brace

1936

Gone with the Wind, by Margaret Mitchell. Macmillan
The Last Puritan, by George Santayana. Scribner

1937

Gone with the Wind, by Margaret Mitchell. Macmillan
Northwest Passage, by Kenneth Roberts. Doubleday, Doran

1938

The Yearling, by Marjorie Kinnan Rawlings. Scribner
The Citadel, by A. J. Cronin. Little, Brown

1939

The Grapes of Wrath, by John Steinbeck. Viking Press
All This, and Heaven Too, by Rachel Field. Macmillan

1940

How Green Was My Valley, by Richard Llewellyn. Macmillan
Kitty Foyle, by Christopher Morley. Lippincott.

1941

The Keys of the Kingdom, by A. J. Cronin. Little, Brown
Random Harvest, by James Hilton. Little, Brown

1942

The Song of Bernadette, by Franz Werfel. Viking Press
The Moon Is Down, by John Steinbeck. Viking Press

1943

The Robe, by Lloyd C. Douglas. Houghton Mifflin
The Valley of Decision, by Marcia Davenport. Scribner

1944

Strange Fruit, by Lillian Smith. Reynal & Hitchcock
The Robe, by Lloyd C. Douglas. Houghton Mifflin

1945

Forever Amber, by Kathleen Winsor. Macmillan
The Robe, by Lloyd C. Douglas. Houghton Mifflin

1946

The King's General, by Daphne du Maurier. Doubleday
This Side of Innocence, by Taylor Caldwell. Scribner

1947

The Miracle of the Bells, by Russell Janney. Prentice-Hall
The Moneyman, by Thomas B. Costain. Doubleday

1948

The Big Fisherman, by Lloyd C. Douglas. Houghton Mifflin
The Naked and the Dead, by Norman Mailer. Rinehart

1949

The Egyptian, by Mika Waltari. Putnam
The Big Fisherman, by Lloyd C. Douglas. Houghton Mifflin

1950

The Cardinal, by Henry Morton Robinson. Simon & Schuster
Joy Street, by Frances Parkinson Keyes. Messner

1951

From Here to Eternity, by James Jones. Scribner
The Caine Mutiny, by Herman Wouk. Doubleday

1952

The Silver Chalice, by Thomas B. Costain. Doubleday
The Caine Mutiny, by Herman Wouk. Doubleday

1953

The Robe, by Lloyd C. Douglas. Houghton Mifflin
The Silver Chalice, by Thomas B. Costain. Doubleday

1954

Not As a Stranger, by Morton Thompson. Scribner
Mary Anne, by Daphne du Maurier. Doubleday

1955

Marjorie Morningstar, by Herman Wouk. Doubleday
Auntie Mame, by Patrick Dennis. Vanguard Press

1956

Don't Go Near the Water, by William Brinkley. Random House
The Last Hurrah, by Edwin O'Connor. Little, Brown

1957

By Love Possessed, by James Gould Cozzens. Harcourt, Brace
Peyton Place, by Grace Metalious. Messner

1958

Doctor Zhivago, by Boris Pasternak. Pantheon Books
Anatomy of a Murder, by Robert Traver. St. Martin's Press

1959

Exodus, by Leon Uris. Doubleday
Doctor Zhivago, by Boris Pasternak. Pantheon Books

1960

Advise and Consent, by Allen Drury. Doubleday
Hawaii, by James A. Michener. Random House

1961

The Agony and the Ecstasy, by Irving Stone. Doubleday
Franny and Zooey, by J. D. Salinger. Little, Brown

1962

Ship of Fools, by Katherine Anne Porter. Little, Brown
Dearly Beloved, by Anne Morrow Lindbergh. Harcourt, Brace &
World

1963

The Shoes of the Fisherman, by Morris L. West. Morrow
The Group, by Mary McCarthy. Harcourt, Brace & World

1964

The Spy Who Came in From the Cold, by John Le Carre. Coward-McCann
Candy, by Terry Southern and Mason Hoffenberg. Putnam

1965

The Source, by James A. Michener. Random House
Up the Down Staircase, by Bel Kaufman. Prentice-Hall

1966

Valley of the Dolls, by Jacqueline Susann. Bernard Geis
The Adventurers, by Harold Robbins. Trident Press

1967

The Arrangement, by Elia Kazan. Stein & Day
The Confessions of Nat Turner, by William Styron. Random
    House
The Chosen, by Chaim Potok. Simon & Schuster

1968

Airport, by Arthur Hailey. Doubleday
Couples, by John Updike. Knopf

1969

Portnoy's Complaint, by Philip Roth. Random House
The Godfather, by Mario Puzo. Putnam

1970

Love Story, by Erich Segal. Harper & Row
The French Lieutenant's Woman, by John Fowles. Little, Brown

1971

Wheels, by Arthur Hailey. Doubleday
The Exorcist, by William P. Blatty. Harper & Row

1972

Jonathan Livingston Seagull, by Richard Bach. Macmillan
August, 1914, by Alexander Solzhenitsyn. Farrar, Straus & Giroux

1973

Jonathan Livingston Seagull, by Richard Bach. Macmillan
Once Is Not Enough, by Jacqueline Susann. Morrow.

1974

Centennial, by James A. Michener. Random House.
Watership Down, by Richard Adams. Macmillan.

NONFICTION

1912

The Promised Land, by Mary Antin. Houghton Mifflin
The Montessori Method, by Maria Montessori. Stokes

1913

Crowds, by Gerald Stanley Lee. Doubleday, Page
Germany and the Germans, by Price Collier. Scribner

1917

Rhymes of a Red Cross Man, by Robert W. Service. Barse & Hopkins
The First Hundred Thousand, by Ian Hay. Houghton Mifflin (classified by
  PW as a war book)

1918

Rhymes of a Red Cross Man, by Robert W. Service. Barse & Hopkins
My Four Years in Germany, by James W. Gerard. Doran (classified by *PW*
  as a war book)

1919

The Education of Henry Adams, by Henry Adams. Houghton Mifflin
The Years Between, by Rudyard Kipling. Doubleday, Page

1920

Now It Can Be Told, by Philip Gibbs. Harper
The Economic Consequences of the Peace, by John Maynard Keynes. Harcourt, Brace

1921

The Outline of History, by H. G. Wells. Macmillan
White Shadows in the South Seas, by Frederick O'Brien. Century

1922

The Outline of History, by H. G. Wells. Macmillan
The Story of Mankind, by Hendrik Willem Van Loon. Boni & Liveright

1923

Etiquette, by Emily Post. Funk & Wagnalls
The Life of Christ, by Giovanni Papini. Harcourt, Brace

1924

Diet and Health, by Lulu Hunt Peters. Reilly & Lee
The Life of Christ, by Giovanni Papini. Harcourt, Brace

1925

Diet and Health, by Lulu Hunt Peters. Reilly & Lee
The Boston Cooking School Cook Book, new ed. by Fannie Farmer. Little,
  Brown

1926

The Man Nobody Knows, by Bruce Barton. Bobbs-Merrill
Why We Behave Like Human Beings, by George A. Dorsey. Harper

1927

The Story of Philosophy, by Will Durant. Simon & Schuster
Napoleon, by Emil Ludwig. Boni & Liveright

1928

Disraeli, by André Maurois. Appleton
Mother India, by Katherine Mayo. Harcourt, Brace

1929

The Art of Thinking, by Ernest Dimnet. Simon & Schuster
Henry the Eighth, by Francis Hackett. Liveright

1930

The Story of San Michele, by Axel Munthe. Dutton
The Strange Death of President Harding, by Gaston B. Means and May
  Dixon Thacker. Guild Publishing Corp.

1931

Education of a Princess, by Grand Duchess Marie. Viking Press
The Story of San Michele, by Axel Munthe. Dutton

1932

The Epic of America, by James Truslow Adams. Little, Brown
Only Yesterday, by Frederick Lewis Allen. Harper

1933

Life Begins at Forty, by Walter B. Pitkin. Whittlesey House
Marie Antoinette, by Stefan Zweig. Viking Press

1934

While Rome Burns, by Alexander Woollcott. Viking Press
Life Begins at Forty, by Walter B. Pitkin. Whittlesey House

1935

North to the Orient, by Anne Morrow Lindbergh. Harcourt, Brace
While Rome Burns, by Alexander Woollcott. Viking Press

1936

Man the Unknown, by Alexis Carrel. Harper
Wake Up and Live!, by Dorothea Brande. Simon & Schuster

1937

How to Win Friends and Influence People, by Dale Carnegie. Simon & Schuster
An American Doctor's Odyssey, by Victor Heiser. Norton

1938

The Importance of Living, by Lin Yutang. John Day
With Malice Toward Some, by Margaret Halsey. Simon & Schuster

1939

Days of Our Years, by Pierre van Paassen. Hillman-Curl
Reaching for the Stars, by Nora Waln. Little, Brown

1940

I Married Adventure, by Osa Johnson. Lippincott
How to Read a Book, by Mortimer Adler. Simon & Schuster

1941

Berlin Diary, by William L. Shirer. Knopf
The White Cliffs, by Alice Duer Miller. Coward-McCann

1942

See Here, Private Hargrove, by Marion Hargrove. Holt
Mission to Moscow, by Joseph E. Davies. Simon & Schuster

1943

Under Cover, by John Roy Carlson. Dutton
One World, by Wendell L. Willkie. Simon & Schuster

1944

I Never Left Home, by Bob Hope. Simon & Schuster; Home Guide
Brave Men, by Ernie Pyle. Holt

1945

Brave Men, by Ernie Pyle. Holt
Dear Sir, by Juliet Lowell. Duell, Sloan & Pearce

1946

The Egg and I, by Betty MacDonald. Lippincott
Peace of Mind, by Joshua L. Liebman. Simon & Schuster

1947

Peace of Mind, by Joshua L. Liebman. Simon & Schuster
Information Please Almanac, 1947, ed. by John Kieran. Garden City Publishing Co.

1948

Crusade in Europe, by Dwight D. Eisenhower. Doubleday
How to Stop Worrying and Start Living, by Dale Carnegie. Simon & Schuster

1949

White Collar Zoo, by Clare Barnes, Jr. Doubleday
How to Win at Canasta, by Oswald Jacoby. Doubleday

1950

Betty Crocker's Picture Cook Book. McGraw-Hill
The Baby. Simon & Schuster

1951

Look Younger, Live Longer, by Gaylord Hauser. Farrar, Straus & Young
Betty Crocker's Picture Cook Book. McGraw-Hill

1952

The Holy Bible: Revised Standard Version. Nelson
A Man Called Peter, by Catherine Marshall. McGraw-Hill

1953

The Holy Bible: Revised Standard Version. Nelson
The Power of Positive Thinking, by Norman Vincent Peale. Prentice-Hall

1954

The Holy Bible: Revised Standard Version. Nelson
The Power of Positive Thinking, by Norman Vincent Peale. Prentice Hall

1955

Gift from the Sea, by Anne Morrow Lindbergh. Pantheon Books
The Power of Positive Thinking, by Norman Vincent Peale. Prentice-Hall

1956

Arthritis and Common Sense, Revised Edition, by Dan Dale Alexander. Witkower Press

Webster's New World Dictionary of the American Language. Concise Edition, edited by David B. Guralnik. World Publishing Co.

1957

Kids Say the Darndest Things!, by Art Linkletter. Prentice-Hall

The FBI Story, by Don Whitehead. Random House

1958

Kids Say the Darndest Things!, by Art Linkletter. Prentice-Hall

'Twixt Twelve and Twenty, by Pat Boone. Prentice-Hall

1959

'Twixt Twelve and Twenty, by Pat Boone. Prentice-Hall

Folk Medicine, by D. C. Jarvis. Holt

1960

Folk Medicine, by D. C. Jarvis. Holt

Better Homes and Gardens First Aid for Your Family. Meredith Publishing Co.

1961

The New English Bible: The New Testament. Cambridge University Press and Oxford University Press

The Rise and Fall of the Third Reich, by William L. Shirer. Simon & Schuster

1962

Calories Don't Count, by Dr. Herman Taller. Simon & Schuster

The New English Bible: The New Testament. Cambridge University Press and Oxford University Press

1963

Happiness Is a Warm Puppy, by Charles M. Schulz. Determined Productions

Security Is a Thumb and a Blanket, by Charles M. Schulz. Determined Productions

1964

Four Days, by American Heritage and United Press International. Simon & Schuster

I Need All the Friends I Can Get, by Charles M. Schulz. Determined Productions

1965

How To Be a Jewish Mother, by Dan Greenburg. Price/Stern/Sloan
A Gift of Prophecy, by Ruth Montgomery. Morrow

1966

How to Avoid Probate, by Norman F. Dacey. Crown
Human Sexual Response, by William H. Masters and Virginia E. Johnson. Little Brown

1967

Death of a President, by William Manchester. Harper & Row
Misery Is a Blind Date, by Johnny Carson. Doubleday

1968

Better Homes and Gardens New Cook Book. Meredith Press
The Random House Dictionary of the English Language: College Edition. Random House

1969

American Heritage Dictionary of the English Language, William Morris, Editor-in-Chief. Houghton Mifflin
In Someone's Shadow, by Rod McKuen. Random House

1970

Everything You Wanted to Know About Sex but Were Afraid to Ask, by David Reuben, M.D. McKay
The New English Bible. Oxford University Press and Cambridge University Press

1971

The Sensuous Man, by "M". Lyle Stuart
Bury My Heart at Wounded Knee, by Dee Brown. Holt, Rinehart & Winston

1972

The Living Bible, by Kenneth Taylor. Doubleday
I'm O.K., You're O.K., by Thomas Harris. Harper & Row

1973

The Living Bible, by Kenneth Taylor. Doubleday and Tyndale House
Dr. Atkins' Diet Revolution, by Robert C. Atkins. McKay

1974

Total Woman, by Marabel Morgan. Revell
All the President's Men, by Bob Woodward and Carl Bernstein. Simon
& Schuster

PAPERBACKS

1957 *Peyton Place*, by Grace Metalious. Dell
1958 *Peyton Place*, by Grace Metalious. Dell
1959 *Anatomy of a Murder*, by Robert Traver. Dell
1960 *The Untouchables*, by Elliot Ness and Oscar Fraley. Popular Library
1961 *Jacqueline Kennedy*, by Deane and David Heller. Monarch Books
1962 *Catch-22*, by Joseph Heller. Dell
1963 *Lord of the Flies*, by William Golding. Capricorn Books
1964 *On Her Majesty's Secret Service*, by Ian Fleming. New American Library
1965 *The Spy Who Came in from the Cold*, by John Le Carre. Dell
1966 *Up the Down Staircase*, by Bel Kaufman. Avon
1967 *Valley of the Dolls*, by Jacqueline Susann. Bantam
1968 *Rosemary's Baby*, by Ira Levin. Dell
1969 *Airport*, by Arthur Hailey. Bantam Books
1970 *Love Story*, by Erich Segal. New American Library
1971 *Love Story*, by Erich Segal. New American Library
1972 *The Happy Hooker*, by Xaviera Hollander. Dell
1973 *Jonathan Livingston Seagull*, by Richard Bach. Avon
1974 *The Exorcist*, by William P. Blatty. Bantam

V

The Future of Bookselling

by G. Roysce Smith

Executive Director
American Booksellers Association

The future of bookselling depends on the future of books, about which there is from time to time a flurry of doubt. Technologies, pre-TV and post-twentieth century, including the ingestion of knowledge by wafers, have frequently been proposed as menaces to the written word.

Today, with material shortages, energy crises, and price increases common causes for alarm, there is perhaps more justification for concern about the future of the book as the physical object which we presently know. But more goes into a book than materials. A book is more than the product of energy, more than a result of economics. A book is also the coming together of social and cultural forces, and for a mere bookseller to predict what these forces may be even ten years from now is indeed presumptuous.

Yet it is a fact that books have been around a while, and there is no new technology immediately available to challenge their appeal to our senses. Nor is there an imminent technocracy in the wings waiting to control our senses. Indeed, it would appear that George Orwell's *1984* is less prophetic than Walker Percy's *Love in the Ruins.* we seem to be less in danger of being run than of simply running down.

In spite of prophesies, something always happens. When the dust settles, things seem not to have changed very profoundly after all. We *are* in a crisis or, more exactly, several crises. During the seventy-five year history of ABA we have been through many crises, within the industry and without, but our problems seem to have altered but little. Book clubs and world wars, paperback revolutions and student protests, book burnings and the misuse of the Presidency command our attention from time to time. Yet the non-crisis, historical problems of the industry continue: distribution; overproduction of titles; pricing; returns; competition by the publisher with the retailer for the consumer's business; a confusion of terms under which the multitude of publishers do business; shrinkages. While grand and mean things occupy the large stage, the details of life go on.

It is not likely that the details will change much during the next seventy-five years of ABA, although the emphasis on which are the most pressing problems at any given time will. Which is not to say that retail bookselling hasn't gone through some dramatic changes in the past twenty-five years. It is largely the superficial changes which have created the drama while the less immediately visible changes will have the most profound and long-lasting effects.

The most dramatic retailing change of the past decade has been the growth of the gigantic chains, particularly Waldenbooks and B. Dalton, which between them have opened over 500 bookstores in an amazingly short time. The immediate reaction to this startling growth was apprehension on the part of booksellers and publishers alike that this growth would be accomplished at the expense of the independent bookseller.

This way of looking at things proved to be wrong, for it concerned itself with surfaces. The real effect of chains has been to create more customers for books and to inspire existing booksellers to become more aggressive.

The chains created more customers for books by opening in locations which had not been considered prime for book sales before, high traffic locations which attracted new kinds of customers not previously given to buying books, by removing the barrier of a formal entrance to the bookstore, and by bringing more advertising and promotional money into a market area than had previously been spent merchandising books.

The chains inspired existing booksellers to become more aggressive in their own merchandising and, in their efforts to find the money to do this, to become more efficient. They also caused booksellers to look into whether a multi-store operation might not be a good idea for the independent bookseller as well as for the corporate giants. The result has been an exciting growth of independent outlets for books.

Adding to this chain-inspired growth of the independents has been an influx of younger booksellers, many of them disillusioned with industrial and corporation life, knowledgeable in the ways of business as many of their predecessors had not been.

It would appear that this growth is not yet at its peak and that the United States, so long short of bookstores, may yet find an adequate book resource in every community of any size. This is one goal of ABA, and we think it is a better way to serve the intellectual, entertainment and cultural needs of America than books by mail or by telegram or by wafer.

However, in their rush for efficiency, booksellers must always keep the intellectual, entertainment and cultural needs of their communities in the fore, or else they will become dull copies of one another. They must return to offering the services which distinguish the bookstore from the supermarket. Distribution of books from their source to the stores must be speeded up so that stores may once again feel secure in their ability to offer fast and accurate special order service to their customers.

In addition to continuing to encourage the growth of full-service bookstores, ABA will expand its educational activities, particularly as they apply to in-store training of personnel. We shall investigate once again the possibility of a national gift certificate program, which has been so successful in Great Britain, where the proceeds have been used to underwrite bookseller education and the promotion of the reading and book-giving habits.

ABA will look into ways to foster book readership and ownership. We shall continue to do battle with self-appointed censors and with censorship-promoting legislation. We shall use and encourage the use of new technologies when they truly offer both speed and economy.

We shall continue to serve our members and, by serving them, the public, who need the written word and who find the book still the one best way for one generation or one era or one man to pass ideas along to another.

President Eisenhower accepts ABA's presentation of books to the White House Library in November 1953. Shaking hands with the President is Allan McMahan, ABA Board chairman; behind them, the committee in charge of the presentation.

John F. Kennedy, the 35th President of the United States, receives a gift of books for the White House Family Library from representatives of ABA. Standing next to the chief executive is ABA's president, Alva H. Parry.

Lyndon Baines Johnson, the 36th President of the United States, accepts the quadrennial gift of books to the White House Family Library. To the President's left is ABA president Louis Epstein, founder of Pickwick Bookshops.

Richard M. Nixon, 37th President of the United States, accepts ABA's quadrennial gift of books to the White House Family Library in 1969. The President used the occasion to publicize his Right to Read program. He is seen here holding the proclamation with the program's director, James Allen.

President Eisenhower is a guest at the ABA convention in Washington in 1963. At the left is Douglas Black, president of Doubleday, the President's publisher; on the right, Allen Dulles, head of the CIA; in the foreground, Doris Thompson, convention chairman.

Former President Truman cuts the ribbon officially opening the ABA convention in Chicago in 1959. Flanking Mr. Truman left to right are Joseph A. Duffy, executive director; Charles B. Anderson, ABA president; H. Joseph Houlihan, ABA Board Chairman; Alexander Wales, head of ABA's International Exhibit.

Adlai Stevenson is a guest of ABA at the convention in Chicago in 1959. Pictured left to right are Alva Parry, a director; Charles B. Anderson, ABA president; Cass Canfield, president of Harper and Row, Mr. Stevenson's publisher; Mr. Stevenson; and Louis Epstein, a director.

Attorney-General Robert Kennedy addressed the convention in 1962. From left to right: Alva Parry, ABA president; Mr. Kennedy; Joseph A. Duffy, ABA executive director; Alexander P. Wales, in charge of ABA's International Exhibit.

Arthur Brentano, founder of the bookstore chain, sits for a portrait head on the occasion of his 83rd birthday in 1941. The sculptor is Peter Hayward.

The Duke of Windsor is the guest of ABA at its convention in Cleveland, 1951. The Duke is followed by Gilbert Goodkind, Executive Secretary.

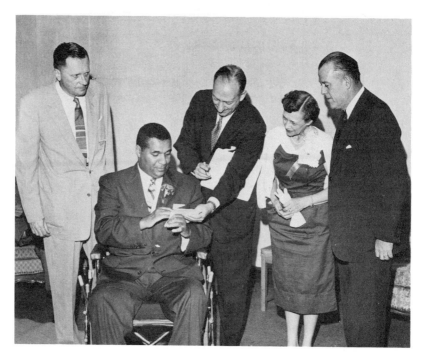

Hall of Fame baseball player and author of It's Good to Be Alive, *Roy Campanella, a speaker at the ABA convention in 1959 in Washington, signs an autograph for Herbert L. Block (cartoonist Herblock), also a speaker. Looking on are Charles B. Anderson, ABA president, Doris Thompson, convention chairman, and Joseph Duffy, ABA executive director.*

Guest speakers at the ABA convention in Chicago, 1960 (left to right): Emmett Dedmon, Chicago Sun-Times; *Theodore White; Phyllis McGinley; William L. Shirer; and H. Joseph Houlihan, convention chairman.*

Dr. Martin Luther King, Jr., guest speaker at the 1967 ABA convention in Washington, talks with Joseph Duffy, executive director, and Emily Sheppard of This Week *magazine.*

Mildred C. Smith, long time editor of Publishers Weekly, *friend and mentor of publishers and booksellers, receiving the Irita Van Doren Award from Joseph A. Duffy, 1968.*

David Frost, popular master of ceremonies on television and author, interviews Maurice Chevalier, one of the most popular entertainers of our time and also an author. The interview took place at the ABA convention in Washington in 1970.

At the ABA convention in Washington in 1974. Standing: Elsa Lichtenstein, Igor Kropotkin, ABA directors; seated: G. Roysce Smith, ABA executive director; actress and author Bette Davis; television emcee and author Dick Cavett.

VI

Shakespeare and Company

by Sylvia Beach

According to a story told by Gertrude Stein, Picasso was once asked by a young man interested in going into the book business where he thought would be the best location in Paris for a new bookstore. "I would just find a place," was Picasso's reply, "and start selling books."

In 1922 Sylvia Beach made literary history when under the imprint of Shakespeare and Company, her bookshop on the left bank in Paris, she published James Joyce's *Ulysses*, which was then banned in every country in the English-speaking world. In the engaging account which follows, excerpted from her autobiography *Shakespeare and Company*, now out of print, she tells how with considerable help and encouragement from her French bookseller friend, Adrienne Monnier, she got started selling and renting books in Paris, just a year after the end of World War I. Her little shop quickly became the meeting place for Americans prominent in the literary world, Ernest Hemingway, Ezra Pound, Gertrude Stein, Scott Fitzgerald and many others. Not a few French writers also became her customers and boosters, among whom were Paul Valéry, Jules Romains, André Gide and André Maurois. For her services to literature Miss Beach in 1936 was awarded the French Legion of Honor and in 1959 the degree of Doctor of Literature by the University of Buffalo. Miss Beach died in 1962.

A Bookshop of My Own

I had long wanted a bookshop, and by now it had become an obsession. I dreamed of a French bookshop but it was to be a branch of Adrienne's and in New York. I wanted to help the French writers I admired so much to become more widely known in my country. I soon realized, however, that my mother's little savings, which she was willing to risk on my venture, would be insufficient to cover the cost of a shop in New York. Very regretfully, I had to abandon this fascinating idea.

I thought Adrienne Monnier would be disappointed to hear of the downfall of our scheme of a French place, a branch of hers, in my country. On the contrary, she was delighted. And so, in a minute, was I, as right before our eyes my bookshop turned into an American one in Paris. My capital would go much further there. Rents were lower and so was the cost of living in those days.

I saw all these advantages. Moreover, I was extremely fond of Paris, I must confess, and this was no small inducement to settle down there and become a Parisian. Then, too, Adrienne had had four years of experience as a bookseller. She had opened her shop in the midst of a war and moreover, kept it going. She promised to advise me in my first steps; also to send me lots of customers. The French, as I knew, were very eager to get hold of our new writers, and it seemed to me that a little American bookshop on the Left Bank would be welcome.

The difficulty was to find a vacant shop in Paris. I might have had to wait some time before finding what I wanted if Adrienne hadn't noticed that there was a place for rent in the rue Dupuytren, a little street just around the corner from the rue de l'Odéon. Busy though she was with her library, her publications, and her own writing, she somehow found time to help me with my preparations. We hurried to the rue Dupuytren, where, at No.8—there were only about ten numbers in this hilly little street—was a shop with the shutters up and a sign saying *"Boutique à louer."* It had once been a laundry, said Adrienne, pointing to the words *"gros"* and *"fin"* on either side of the door, meaning they did up both sheets and fine linen. Adrienne, who was rather plump, placed herself under the *"gros"* and told me to stand under the *"fin"*. "That's you and me," she said.

We hunted up the concierge, an old lady in a black lace cap, who lived in a sort of cage between two floors, as concierges do in these old Paris houses, and showed us the premises. *My* premises, as, without hesitation, I decided they would be. There were two rooms, with a glass door between them, and steps leading into the one at the back. There was a fireplace in the front room; the laundress's stove, with the irons on it, had stood in front of it.

These premises—including the dear old concierge, "la Mère Garrouste," as everyone called her, the kitchenette off the back room, and Adrienne's glass door—everything delighted me, not to mention the very low rent, and I went away to think it over. Mère Garrouste was to think me over, too, for a day or two, according to the best French custom.

Shortly, my mother in Princeton, New Jersey, got a cable from me, saying simply: "Opening bookshop in Paris. Please send money," and she sent me all her savings.

Setting Up Shop

It was great fun getting my little shop ready for the book business. I took the advice of my friends the Wright-Worthings, who had the antique shop Aladdin's Lamp in the rue des Saints Pères, and covered the rather damp walls with sackcloth. A hump-backed upholsterer did this for me, and was very proud of the fluting with which he finished off the corners. A carpenter put up shelves and made over the windows for the books to be displayed in, and a painter came to do the few feet of shop front. He called it the "façade," and promised it would be as fine when he finished it as that of the Bazar de l'Hôtel de Ville, his latest triumph. Then a "specialist" came and painted the name "Shakespeare and Company" across the front. That name came to me one night as I lay in bed. My "Partner Bill," as my friend Penny O'Leary called him, was always, I felt, well disposed toward my undertaking; and, besides, he was a best seller.

Charles Winzer, a Polish-English friend of Adrienne's, made the signboard, a portrait of Shakespeare, to be hung outside. Adrienne didn't approve of the idea, but I wanted it anyway. The signboard hung from a bar above the door. I took it down at night. Once, I forgot it, and it was stolen. Winzer made another, which also disappeared. Adrienne's sister made a third one, a rather French-looking Shakespeare, which I still have.

Now perhaps some people wouldn't know what a "Bookhop" is. Well, that's what the specialist carefully spelled out above the window at the right, opposite the words "Lending Library." I let "Bookhop" remain for a while. It quite described Shakespeare and Company making its début in bookselling.

All these artisans, in spite of their interest in the place, were extremely intermittent in their attendance. Sometimes I wondered if they wouldn't still be busy there on the opening day, upholstering, doing carpentry, and painting the place. At least the shop, so full of people, would look bustling.

The "office furniture" in my shop was all antique. A charming mirror and a gate-legged table came from the Wright-Worthings, the rest from the flea market, where you really found bargains in those days.

The books in my lending library, except for the latest, came from the well-stocked English secondhand bookstores in Paris. They, too, were antiques, some of them far too valuable to be circulated; and if the members of my library hadn't been so honest, many, instead of a few, of the volumes would soon have been missing from the shelves. The fascinating bookshop near the Bourse, Boiveau and Chevillet, which has disappeared now, was a field of discovery for excavators who were willing to go down into the cellar, holding a lighted candle provided by dear old Monsieur Chevillet himself—what a risk!—and dig up the treasures buried under layers of stuff.

[My sister] Cyprian, who was in the United States just then, sent me the latest American books. I went over to London and brought back two trunks full of English books, mostly poetry. Mrs. Alida Monro, who with Harold Monro ran the Poetry Bookshop, a wonderful place, very kindly gave me a great deal of information on the subject of poetry publications and how to procure them. And I went around to see the publishers. All of them were most courteous and encouraging about the new bookshop in Paris, and gave me every facility, though, for all they knew, I might be an adventuress. In fact, so I was.

On the way to the boat train, I stopped in Cork Street at the little bookshop of the publisher and bookseller Elkin Mathews to order my Yeats, Joyce, and Pound. He was sitting in a sort of gallery, with books surging around and creeping up almost to his feet. We had a pleasant talk, and he was quite friendly. I mentioned seeing some drawings by William Blake—if only I could have something of Blake's in my shop! Thereupon he produced two beautiful original drawings, which he sold to me for a sum that, according to Blake experts who saw them later, was absurdly small.

Shakespeare and Company Opens Its Doors

Instead of writing down the titles I wanted from Elkin Mathews —indeed, I hadn't time, and anyway we understood each other so well—I gave him a flying order for Yeats, Joyce, and Pound, and for any portraits he might have of them around the shop. A few days later, in Paris, a huge sack arrived from Elkin Mathews. It contained the works I had ordered, and also dozens of what the French call *"rossignols"*, a poetic name for unsalable items. Obviously, it was a good chance to dump these birds on me. Besides the books, the sack contained some enormous portraits: at least half a dozen of Byron; the rest of Nelson, Wellington, and other characters in English history. Judging by their size, they were intended for the walls of official buildings. I sent them back and scolded Elkin Mathews severely. Still, because of the Blakes, I didn't hold it against him; and I have only pleasant memories of the old gentleman. . . .

Instead of setting a date for the opening of my bookshop, I decided that I would simply open it as soon as it was ready.

Finally, the day came when all the books I could afford were on the shelves, and one could walk around the shop without falling over ladders and buckets of paint. Shakespeare and Company opened its doors. The day was November 19, 1919. It had taken me since August to reach this point. In the windows were displayed the works of our Patron, of Chaucer, of T. S. Eliot, Joyce, and so on. There was also Adrienne's favorite English book, *Three Men in a Boat.* Inside, a review rack held copies of the *Nation,* the *New Republic,* the *Dial,* the *New Masses, Playboy,* the *Chapbook,* the *Egoist,* the *New English Review,* and other literary magazines. On the walls, I had put up my two Blake drawings, and photographs of Whitman and Poe. Then there were two photographs of Oscar Wilde, in velvet breeches and cloak. They were framed with some of Wilde's letters that a friend of Cyprian's, Byron Kuhn, had given me. Also on display were several little manuscripts of Walt Whitman scribbled on the backs of letters. . . .

A good many friends had been waiting for the opening of Shakespeare and Company; and the news got around that the time had come. Still, I didn't really expect to see anybody that day. And just as well, I thought. I would need twenty-four hours to realize this Shakespeare and Company bookshop. But the shutters in which the little shop went to bed every night were hardly removed (by a waiter from a nearby café) when the first friends began to turn up. From that moment on, for over twenty years, they never gave me time to meditate.

Lending books, just as I had foreseen, was much easier in Paris than selling them. The only cheap editions of English writers were the Tauchnitz and the Conrad, and they didn't go much further than Kipling and Hardy in those days. Our moderns, particularly when pounds and dollars were translated into francs, were luxuries the French and my Left Bankers were not able to afford. That is why I was interested in my lending library. So I got everything I liked myself, to share with others in Paris.

My lending library was run on what Adrienne called, though I never knew why, *"le plan américain."* It would have horrified an American librarian, with her catalogues and card indexes and mechanical appliances. It was quite suitable for a library such as mine. There was no catalogue—I preferred to let people find out for themselves how much was lacking; no card index—so unless you could remember, as Adrienne, with her wonderful memory, was able to do, to whom all your books were lent, you had to look through all the members' cards to find out what had become of a volume.

There were, to be sure, the large cards, each bearing the name and address of the member, the date of subscription, the amount of the subscription plus the deposit, and, of course, the title of the book he or she took out. Or books. A member could take out one or two volumes, could change them whenever he liked or keep them a fortnight. (Joyce took out dozens, and sometimes kept them for years.) Each member had a small identity card, which he was supposed to produce when claiming the deposit at the expiration of his subscription, or when he was broke. This membership card was as good as a passport, so I was told.

One of the first members . . . who came along was Gide. I saw Adrienne Monnier coming around the corner from the rue de l'Odéon escorting him. It was just like Gide to hurry up and encourage me in my undertaking. I was always timid in Gide's presence, though Adrienne said "Pooh!" when I told her; and now, rather overwhelmed by the honor, I wrote on a card: "André Gide: I, Villa Montmorency, Paris XVI; 1 year; 1 volume," making a big blot as I did so.

Gide was tall and handsome. He wore a broad-brimmed Stetson, and I saw a resemblance to William S. Hart. He wore a cape or a sort of Teddy bear coat over his shoulders, and, with his height, he was impressive as he strode along. Gide continued to take an interest in Shakespeare and Company and its proprietor all through the years.

André Maurois was also one of the first to bring me his good wishes. And he brought me a copy of his newly published little masterpiece, *Les Silences du Colonel Bramble*.

Pilgrims from America

I was too far from my country to follow closely the struggles of the writers there to express themselves, and I didn't foresee, when I opened my bookshop in 1919, that it was going to profit by the suppressions across the sea. I think it was partly to these suppressions, and the atmosphere they created, that I owed many of my customers—all those pilgrims of the twenties who crossed the ocean and settled in Paris and colonized the Left Bank of the Seine.

The news of my bookshop, to my surprise, soon spread all over the United States, and it was the first thing the pilgrims looked up in Paris. They were all customers at Shakespeare and Company, which many looked upon as their club. Often, they would inform me that they had given Shakespeare and Company as their address, and they hoped I didn't mind. I didn't, especially since it was too late to do anything about it except to try to run an important mailing office as efficiently as possible.

VII

Bookselling in Boston

by Frederic G. Melcher

The late Frederic G. Melcher, for many years president of the R. R. Bowker Co. and one of the most renowned and beloved of American publishers, was originally a bookseller. At the age of sixteen he took a job in Boston with Estes and Lauriat, later the Charles E. Lauriat Co., and remained there for eighteen years. He then moved to Indianapolis, Indiana, to become the manager of the W. K. Stewart Bookstore, during which time he was also an officer of ABA. In a speech delivered in 1956 before the American Antiquarian Society, excerpted here, he tells of his early days in Boston.

In these present days of vocational preparation and careful career decisions, my entrance by pure chance into the book business seems haphazard. I had prepared for Massachusetts Tech at Newton High School, but at the last moment had turned firmly against science. Jobs were scarce in 1895 as the business cycle was at one of its low ebbs because of the "panic of '93" and the silver tide threatening from the West. I had no inherited interest in, and no evident wisdom as to books, but I considered myself fortunate, at the age of sixteen, to find a job at Lauriat's Bookstore in Boston. As a beginner I had charge of handling the incoming and outgoing mail (letters copied with the aid of moist blotters and a screw press); the recording of staff arrival time, 8 to 6, six days a week; and answering the wall telephone, the first one I had used regularly in all my sixteen years. The going pay for beginners was $4.00 a week.

Bookselling had always been learned by apprenticeship, un-

At the ABA convention in Chicago, in 1957, Frederic G. Melcher (left) receives the ABA Award of Merit from H. Joseph Houlihan, ABA president 1956–58.

less by hardy adventuring, and, perhaps, I was lucky to begin at an early age, as it gave me plenty of time to proceed gradually through the different activities of the business and to try a hand, in this fine old shop, at everything but store management, which I was to try later at Indianapolis.

The Lauriat bookstore was at the central point of five Washington Street bookstores. Little, Brown was at the northern end of the row in a wide store which ran through to Devonshire Street. The publishing department was in the mezzanine. Its immense success with *Quo Vadis* had taken the firm's attention away from the retail business, but careful and competent service was given to a steady trade.

Across the street from Little, Brown at School Street was the famous Old Corner Bookstore. It was a store of alert service and the sharpest new book competition for Lauriat's. There was a big magazine counter that brought a steady stream of customers. It has seemed too bad that that old building with its great Ticknor and Fields and E. P. Dutton traditions could not always have remained a bookstore. There is no such bookstore tradition anywhere in the country, and it is almost as well known as a landmark as the Old State House and the Old South Church and located half way between these two shrines. The name has been kept, but two moves have served to dissolve the inherited atmosphere.

One hundred yards south of Lauriat's was DeWolfe Fiske and Company. One half of the store was open to the street, which gave it the name of Archway Bookstore. How the dust did blow in on those bargain books, keeping Mr. Fiske busy with his big feather duster.

Opposite DeWolfe's was William B. Clarke and Company, which supplemented its income with a leadership in social stationery and a big rental library. Clarke was the doughtiest fighter in the country for "fair trade" pricing in the booksellings. A man with a cause, a valiant spirit who wore himself out and his business down in that cause, he saw clearly that good book distribution depended on price stabilization.

Still one other type of book outlet should not be forgotten, the fairly recently developing book departments of Jordan's and White's, who, in the department store practice of that day, used cut-prices on popular current books to bring customers to the white goods or other profitable departments.

The Lauriat Bookstore at which I arrived every morning from Newton Center at eight had an unimpressive front of fifteen feet, two show windows, one devoted to the old and rare stock and the other to current books. Under one side was a sidewalk-level window which swung open to let in the wooden cases and bundles of arriving books or to let shipments out. Coal for the one central hot-air furnace was poured down through a manhole.

The long, narrow store widened a bit farther in, and in the rear, under the skylight, doubled in size. Dark oak bookcases ran the full length of the store with secondary rows for books along the back of each shelf. Book-width ledges were three feet from the floor with bins below. The flat counters of heavy oak ran both sides of a main aisle and so near to the shelves that customers felt like intruders if they went back to browse. The counters had broad drawers that might house picture books, prayerbooks and hymnals, or perhaps were used for the cloth sheets that were thrown over every counter at night before the store was swept out.

*Charles E. Lauriat (1842–1920) was president of the
Charles E. Lauriat Co. in Boston from 1899 to 1920.*

At the end of the counters were small stand-up desks for the salesmen to keep sale memorandums and customer lists; behind them were two roll-top desks with their well-stuffed pigeon-holes, used by two of Mr. Lauriat's assistants. At the aisle's end behind a swinging gate was Mr. Lauriat's roll-top. Each roll-top was locked at night. In the flat upper drawer of Mr. Lauriat's desk was the daily sales record at which we took anxious looks, for a salesman's reputation, and consequently, his future income, depended on those figures. There were also a shipping counter and a cashier's cage. Then, against the back wall, the built-in desk where I began work.

I was shortly moved from the mail desk to a more bookish job in the basement as the receiver for all incoming stock, new books and old. The expressman dropped his big wooden cases or bundles on the sidewalk outside, pushed a bell, the swinging window opened, and up and down the wooden slide came case after case. Daily shipments came from New York via the Stonington Line, and on occasion, great shipments of fifty to a hundred cases from London. If one was to know books, this was the job. There were, in two years, tens of thousands of books into which I pencilled cost and selling marks (the code word was "Cumberland" for the ten digits), checked the bills and saw the books to stock. I so liked the daily handling of the infinitely varied content of incoming cases and bundles that I almost regretted later to be taken upstairs to handle, first, mail orders, then library shipments.

Lauriat's did not have departments for stationery, magazines or cards, but did have books of wide variety, the so-called standard sets that are not commonly seen in bookstores today. The demand for standard books in uniform sets has fallen off steadily, but at that time it was expected to find them in a good bookstore, the Gadshill Dickens, Smith Elder Thackeray, Harper's Hardy, Scribner Stevenson, all the New England authors in the Riverside Editions, the Cambridge Poets, etc., etc. All these editions we knew, and the stock was complete for the buyers of separate volumes. In the great run on Temple Shakespeare in the '90s, the titles, arranged in the order of the First Folio, were renewed almost daily. The whole span of great authors was somewhere on the shelves, and we came to know all the comparative merits of different editions. When the craze for bible-paper flexible leather editions came along, hundreds of people were filling up sets volume by volume, and friend told friend what volumes of Stevenson, Kipling, Austen, they wanted for birthday or Christmas.

Perhaps because of the old Boston clientele we were serving we could sell by the hundreds the Life and Letters of Holmes or Lowell, Morley's Life of Gladstone or Allen's Life of Phillips Brooks, etc. The era of recorded best sellers was just beginning, and our contribution to the totals was to sell in hundred lots *When Knighthood Was in Flower, David Harum, Soldiers of Fortune* and others. It was exciting to see the piles melt away, but the facts of the new book business were such that, because of meeting the price competition, we probably lost money on every current book we sold, and we had to make it up on old English stock and remainders from England. Even back in the 19th century the practice of seeking business by giving some, and finally everyone, a discount had been ingrained in the book business. The $1.50 book was sold at $1.12 or $1.10 in Boston, and the store had paid 90 cents for single copies, 85 cents for 25 or over, 81 cents for lots of 100. Every once in a while a department store would take a leader and sell it to anyone for 85 cents. At whatever the level to the customer you lost money and stores all over the country were giving up or switching to stationery.

The sales value of the jacket had not been discovered at that time but the cloth covers were often in gold stamping design. Novels were usually illustrated, perhaps by Gibson or Christy. Our new fiction counter, the busiest spot in the store, had neat piles in parallel rows. A big seller might be stacked up from a box on the floor. I liked the excitement of selling. Here books were being mated to actual readers, author reputations were being built, personal tastes developed, book audiences being created. If every publisher were to have bookstore experience, he would have valuable knowledge of the ways of the public in its acceptance and resistance of books. To know the book-buying public at its best and worst, one should have gone through a Christmas season at Lauriat's. Two, three, even four customers at a time, quick interpretations of needs and tastes, complete knowledge of the whereabouts of every book in a large stock, 35 cents for supper money, then long evenings for clearing up. I wouldn't have wished to miss the experience, but it was hard.

The books in stock would have been easier to locate, both for salesmen and for customers, I always thought, if they were arranged by subject. But tradition had decided that all the books of each publisher be together. This made it easier to check the catalogues of a publisher on the traveler's semi-annual visit. So if an author had four publishers, you brought them to your customer from four directions. I considered it quite a triumph when I persuaded management to let me put the editions of poetry old and new in one section. My other effort toward departmentalizing was to bring together the books for children. This department had had once-a-year attention only, and the other salesmen cheerfully gave me special rights in seeking to develop year-round service to those parents who gave thought to their children's reading.

The Lauriat clientele were the people of established book-buying habits. Men who were the heaviest buyers would be likely to come up from State and Devonshire Streets, lawyers, financial and insurance men, perhaps dropping in after lunch at Thompson's Spa, Parker House or Young's. Women customers came in from the Back Bay, Brookline, the Newtons, Cambridge and Milton. Harvard provided good buyers, though not as many as I would have expected; however, many of these stayed with us as customers if they moved across country. It sometimes troubled me that we seemed to be developing so few really new book buyers. Our visitors were those with already established reading habits. The parents who were buying children's books were the children of parents who had bought them children's books, Alcott, Hawthorne, Howard Pyle.

The high tide of great New England authors had passed. Thomas Bailey Aldrich, as a last leaf on the tree, used to drop in regularly. Sarah Orne Jewett was a distinguished visitor, a quiet dignified figure, an author marked for permanent esteem. Laura E. Richards, an important author of that time, was a frequent visitor from Maine. Her mother, Julia Ward Howe, was still living. Amy Lowell would telephone her needs, perhaps for out-of-the-way French books. I have met people in different parts of the country who began their book buying in the Boston bookstores of those years.

Boston bookstores have had over the years a real part in making Boston mean books and libraries to tens of thousands of people. My eighteen years in one of Boston's famous stores fell at the turn of the century and at a turning point for the book business of the country. If there is to be increased interest in the story of bookselling, and an active desire to pass on the experience of each generation to the next, informal records like this one of mine may have their place. Such are the evidences, it has been said, of a business evolving into a profession.

VIII

Lo, the Poor Bookseller

by H. L. Mencken

Joseph Lilly, the bookseller, said to a customer on a Saturday afternoon, "Oh, sir, do buy something of me; I have not sold a book this week."

Henry Louis Mencken, co-founder with George Jean Nathan of the magazine *American Mercury,* was during the 1920s and 1930s one of the most influential and acerbic critics of the American scene. For many years he wrote book reviews for the Sun papers in Baltimore. He was the author in the 1930s of *The American Language,* a book that is still a staple in the stores. Of an evening, after a long day's editorial stint, he used to like to relax in one of his favorite haunts, a "Bierstube" in Baltimore which was run as an adjunct to a bookstore. In this article written for the *American Mercury* in 1930, as the country was about to enter its second year of depression, Mr. Mencken takes up his formidable cudgels on behalf of the American bookseller.

I

This is a bad season in the publishing business, as it is in other lines of business in the United States. The advance orders for books on the fall list have run but little beyond half those of last year, and there has been a similar, an even more dramatic, drop in the sale of books already in print. Most of the American publishers, fortunately, seem likely to weather the drought without serious damage, for it follows several seasons of good business and they thus have ample reserves. Moreover, they are so organized that they can cut down at least part of their overhead to meet the shrinkage in sales. But the booksellers, with expensive stores to maintain, are making heavier weather of it, and not a few of them seem to be in serious difficulties. One of the largest of them, in fact, is already in the hands of a creditors' committee, and several others of the first flight have had to ask for extensions. No doubt the collapse of the Hoover prosperity is chiefly to blame for this lamentable state of affairs. Whether rightly or not, the American people believe that hard times are upon them, and in consequence they tend to reduce their expenditures, especially for luxuries. The automobile men have felt the pinch for almost a year past, and so have the hotel men and the steamship men. As for the theatre men, they have their back to the wall, and are fighting, not only for a living, but for life itself. No one, in times of stress does much theatre-going, for the movies are much cheaper and the radio is cheaper still.

The chief burden of all this falls upon the booksellers, for the publishers, as I have said, can go slowly when the going is bad and thus trim their expenditure to meet at least a part of their loss of income. But the bookseller has to keep his store open as usual, and it is hard for him to diminish his overhead. His customers, even the best of them, buy less than usual, but they expect him to maintain the same service. If one of them asks him for this or that book, and he hasn't got it on his shelves, he is apt to lose not only the immediate sale but also future patronage. For the people who read books, taking one with another, are an impatient lot, and do not submit to delays with any grace. When they have to wait five or six days for what seems to them to be a standard book—which means any book they may happen to want at the moment—they put down the bookseller as a merchant who is bad at his business, and begin to say that it would be a good thing if a better one opened across the street.

What this means to the bookseller who pretends to a really dignified position in the trade is that the size of his stock, considered in relation to his annual sales, must always be a large one, and that his investment in it, in consequence, must be relatively unproductive. It means that he must carry at least one copy of nearly every book that any customer who really knows books is apt to ask for. How many such books are in print in the United States I don't know precisely, but some time ago, examining the catalogues of all the American publishers for another purpose, I had a chance to make a rough estimate. My conclusion was that between 4000 and 6000 such books were listed—say 5000 to make it more definite. In other words, every bookseller who pretends to keep a first-rate store must have most of these 5000 standard titles in stock, though many of them sell very slowly and all of them together probably net him less than 10,000 sales a year.

Perhaps I had better illustrate what I mean by standard titles. A good example is Benvenuto Cellini's autobiography. If you went into a bookstore and asked for it, and the bookseller told you that he would have to order it, you'd certainly conclude that he kept a third-rate store. So with any book by Mark Twain, or any play by Ibsen, or any one of Joseph Conrad's novels, or any book by Galsworthy, or H. G. Wells, or Thackeray, or Dostoevski, or O.Henry, or Thomas Mann, or Dreiser, or Carl Sandburg. And so with a vast mass of miscellaneous books—Renan's *Life of Jesus*, Adam Smith's *The Wealth of Nations*, Darwin's *The Origin of Species*, Newman's *Apologia Pro Vita Sua*, the *Spectator*, Boswell's *Life of Johnson*, Mrs. Post's etiquette book, Giles's *Chinese Literature*, Howells's *The Rise of Silas Lapham*, Harris's *Uncle Remus*, Whitman's *Leaves of Grass*, Andrew D. White's *History of the Warfare of Science with Theology in Christendom*, Tolstoi's *War and Peace*, the Koran, Mill's *On Liberty*, Bryce's *American Commonwealth*, Plato's *Republic*. These books are not best-sellers. Even the largest bookstore may go a year or even five years without selling a single copy of any given one of them. But any bookstore that didn't stock most of them would seem a poor thing, and not many habitual readers would patronize it.

What this amounts to in money invested I don't know, but certainly it must be plain that the bookseller suffers from his very slow turn-over and that his net profits must be small. A good part of his stock of standard books, in fact, he probably never sells at all: it remains on his shelves for years, and is then handed over to his successor, or to the receiver in bankruptcy. The books become shopworn; he must keep on reducing them, often to below cost. New editions come out, and displace those he has in hand. Books that are standard today become obsolete tomorrow. And all the while rent, interest, insurance and help hire go on.

II

His actual profits, of course—if he makes any—do not come out of this sort of business. He keeps it out of pride in his business, out of a desire for prestige—perhaps most of all in the hope that keeping it up will draw in another and more lucrative kind of trade. That is the trade in new books.

But here he faces difficulties almost as serious, for nearly 10,000 new books come out in the United States every year. How does he choose among them—for plainly enough he can't stock all of them? He chooses, in the main, by sheer guessing —and unless he guesses with extraordinary luck he is very likely to be stuck. On the one hand, he may not order enough copies of one book to meet its sudden and unexpected sale, and on the other hand he may order too many copies of another book and find them on his hands.

The risk is very real, as every bookseller knows to his woe. Every publishing season is full of surprises and alarms—books that become best-sellers unaccountably and other books that as unaccountably fail. The former sell with a whoop, and the sale is usually over in short order; everyone wants them at once. If the bookseller, having guessed well, has laid in a large supply he may make a quick and big profit. But if, like a good business man, he has discounted his hunch a bit and bought cautiously, he may see scores of customers walk out of his store in a dudgeon, the while he telegraphs frantically (along with 400 or 500 booksellers) for fresh supplies. And when they come in he may discover that even the most eager book-buyers do not hold their libido long, and that the hot demand of last week has been satisfied by borrowing or forgetting.

But what really fetches him is not the book that is an unexpected success, but the book that is an unexpected failure. He has to buy it long in advance—sometimes before it is actually written. If it is to be published in October the drummers may see him as early as May. They are very eloquent fellows, and know how to cry up their goods, even when those goods are still nothing more than vague ideas in the heads of certain godless and perhaps alcoholic authors. The bookseller, succumbing to the rhetoric, orders heavily—and six months later he may have a ton of unsaleable books on his hands, and be sitting up nights trying to figure out a way to induce the publisher to take them back.

In the middle ground, among the books that are neither great successes nor great failures—in other words, among the books that strike a fair average, and give him whatever regular profit he really makes—here in this middle ground he has troubles too. Of a given book, shall he order ten copies or twenty-five? He risks the twenty-five and sells nineteen within a month; then the book dies. He has lost nothing—but his profit is still standing on his shelf. Of another book he orders ten, sells them at once, orders ten more—and has five of them at the end of the year. Settling down bravely for the long, long pull, he lives, perhaps, to see the publisher close out the title as a remainder (at 20 cents on the dollar) to the department-store down the street, or rent the plates to a cheap reprint magnate who loads up the drugstore at the corner.

Is it any wonder that a merchant so beset, when hard times come down to add to his ordinary troubles, tends to be pushed to the wall? The marvel is, indeed, that he ever survives at all. It is as if a haberdasher, in addition to meeting all the hazards of the current fashion, had to keep in stock a specimen of every kind of shirt, collar, sock, necktie and undershirt in favor since 1750. And as if the same haberdasher, in addition to selling against all the other haberdashers in his town, had to face the competition of cut-rate stores selling standard shirts for fifty cents and collars for a nickel.

III

Just what is to be done to rescue the poor bookseller I don't know, but certainly most of the remedies currently proposed are plainly dubious. There is, for example, the remedy of reducing the prices of books—selling new novels, say, for a dollar, and new works of a more "serious" cast at proportionate reductions. Will it do any good? I see little reason to believe so. The theory behind the scheme is that books are now too expensive, and that people would buy more if they were cheaper. Superficially, that may seem to be sound reasoning, but there is really no evidence that books are now too expensive, or that they could be sold profitably at the low prices now talked of. My guess is that cheaper books, if they become more numerous, will simply bring down the bookseller's profit to nothing, and so hasten his bankruptcy. Even with luck, he is making very little now. How can he be expected to make more when his margin is reduced to a few cents?

Already, in fact, he handles a good many very cheap books—perhaps more than he ought to. They are reprints of books that have been sold in the past at higher prices, and are sufficiently well known to command a more or less steady sale. But it is one thing to sell such books, whether in a bookstore or in a drug-store, and quite another thing to sell new books, however low the price, that are quite unknown. This last is what the apostles of cheaper books are asking the bookseller to do. They want him to sell three, four or six times as many copies of a given new book than he can sell now, simply on the ground that the price has been reduced from $2.50 to $1.00. But how he is going to do it they do not say. By inducing his present customers to buy three, four or six times as many books? Or by developing a trade among persons who will buy anything, so long as it is cheap? In neither direction can I see anything awaiting him except more trouble.

The cheap book experiment, in fact, will probably injure the bookseller in another way, for it will tend to lure more and more drug-stores, department-stores, hardware stores, grocery-stores and other such emporia into bookselling, and so drag his customers away from him. People will no longer go to bookstores as they do now, to browse among books and be educated in reading; they will make their selections from meagre and shabby stocks, with piles of camera films to one side and bales of hot-water bags to the other. Buying books will cease to be the pleasant adventure that it has been ever since the invention of printing; instead it will become a kind of vulgar shopping. Perhaps this will be of benefit to the drug-store chains, but how can it bring any good to the bookseller?

I suspect that his salvation (if, indeed, he is ever saved) will lie in specialization. He will become a dealer in *good* books, and leave the trash to his new competitors. He will scrutinize his stock more carefully than in the past, and try to get rid of the dead wood that now encumbers it. He will withdraw from competition with the drug-stores and the news-stands, and make his appeal to readers who are really readers, and not mere idlers. Following the example of his German colleagues, he will address to interesting such readers, directly and promptly, in the new books of genuine merit, and do something to promote his sales in the market where an enlightened will to buy already exists.

Along this route there may be a way out for him. The drug-stores and their like are hurting all booksellers very badly, but they are hurting the incompetent ones a great deal more than they are hurting the good ones. All the horde of vague and silly booke-shoppes, run mainly by female amateurs, will go first. When they are cleared off, the gap separating the first-rate book-store from the cheap-jack book-counter will be wider and plainer than ever, and people who really love and respect books will turn automatically to the former. There will be fewer book-sellers, but they will be delivered at last from a kind of competition that they are not fitted for, and that can only ruin them.

IV

Both publishers and booksellers, in the recent past, have been badly upset by yielding to the current American rumble-bumble about high-pressure salesmanship, mass production and the "creation" of buyers. The gentlemen who now venture upon the large-scale manufacture of cheap books are still under that spell, and will presently, I believe, come to grief. The more prudent publishers will cut down their lists; not a few of them, in fact, are already doing so. Too many books are being published—and especially too many bad books. They pile up absurdly, almost insanely. When I first began reviewing, now nearly a quarter of a century ago, I could make some sort of acquaintance with practically all the new books that came out in the United States each year, discarding the obvious trash. But of late it has been a sheer impossibility. I am lucky if I get my nose into a third of them.

Fewer books would mean not only better books, but better sales for them. As things stand, the bad ones offer heavy and often ruinous competition to the good ones. The same publisher, eager to grab every MS. in sight, publishes books that actually compete with one another and his whooping for one is indistinguishable from his whooping for the rest. No one believes a publisher's recommendation any more, and the blurbs printed on dust-covers, like the prefaces by eminent hands within, have lost all force and effect. The publisher who comes out of the present hard times with the least damage, and faces the revival of business with the best chance of getting a profitable share of it, will be that one who most resolutely purges his list of the meretricious and the unnecessary, and so gives the highest authority and dignity to his imprint.

The booksellers too might very well mend their ways. Some of their troubles are beyond their control, but not all. Too many of them, like the publishers, have got drunk on huge sales. It will do them good to reflect that sales, in themselves, mean little: the important thing is profits. I believe that selling good books, in the long run, is more profitable than selling bad ones—that the high apparent yield from trash is set off by large losses, and that the business, in the last analysis, is a losing one. Some of the drug-stores, I am told, are already finding that out. Perhaps it will take a year or two of experience with bargain books to convince the booksellers. Those who are convinced soonest, I am convinced, will be keeping the bookstores of the United States five years hence. The rest will be working as garage attendants, chiropractors, policemen or bootleggers.

IX

Never Be a Bookseller

by David Garnett

Lord! When you sell a man a book you don't sell him just twelve
ounces of paper and ink and glue—you sell him a whole new life.
Love and friendship and humour and ships at sea by night—
there's all heaven and earth in a book, a real book.

Christopher Morley in *Parnassus on Wheels*

Well-known in Great Britain as both novelist and publisher,
David Garnett in 1930 wrote this account of his bookselling
experience for his friend Adolph Kroch, Chicago bookseller,
who published it in a small edition for free distribution to
friends of the trade.

"Never try to write, but above all never have anything to do
with publishing or the book trade"; this is the only parental
advice that I can remember. My father constantly repeated it, my
mother backed him up, and together they encouraged my interests in everything but literature.

When I decided to become an economic botanist they were
delighted.

"That's splendid! Anything so long as you don't try to live by
writing, publishing or selling books."

The war came and in 1915 I sold my microscope and went out
with my friend Francis Birrell to the Quakers to work in the
Friends' War Victims Relief Expedition. When the war was over,
I had forgotten my science and quite lost interest in it; Birrell
and I were both at a loose end and it was natural that we should
think of starting a bookshop together.

Birrell really knew a lot about books; his father, the Rt. Hon.

Augustine Birrell has a passion for books and a fine library, and his grandfather, Frederick Locker, had formed in the Rowfant Library one of the most wonderful small collections of valuable books in the world—in the days before the millionaires came into the market.

And I may claim to have a certain family connection with books also; my great-grandfather, the Rev. Richard Garnett, was assistant keeper of printed books in the British Museum Library and a great scholar. When he died, Sir Anthony Panizzi took my grandfather, Richard Garnett, into the library at the age of sixteen. He remained there forty-eight years, was keeper of printed books, and was responsible for making and printing the general catalogue—no small job, as booksellers may imagine, since the British Museum Library is the largest collection of books in the world. He also invented and introduced the "sliding press", by which bookcases are stacked solid and can be pulled out endways like books from a shelf.

My father, Edward Garnett, is a literary critic, and has been a publisher's reader for more than forty years, during which time he must have read more manuscripts of novels than anyone alive. My mother, Constance Garnett, has recently seen her seventieth volume of translation from the Russian in print and declares that she will not translate another—but she may change her mind.

But though I had been brought up among an edifying confusion of books, manuscripts and dictionaries, and had known a good many distinguished writers all my life, I knew practically nothing about the book trade. Birrell and I took a room in an out-of-the-way street and launched out into selling books, new and secondhand, English and foreign, deciding to do everything, all at once, on a capital of four thousand dollars.

Our education began: we learnt where to buy string and kraft paper and how to do up parcels. We attended auctions of second-hand books and I went to country sales.

It was some time before customers came to our shop, but we slowly collected a stock of books, issued a catalogue of our old books, and spent a lot of time running round to the different publishers and queuing up with the collectors . . .

We did not employ an assistant and worked really hard and certainly earned the fifteen dollars a week we each drew as wages.

We soon learned that a bookseller selling new books has to work unbelievably hard, that half the time he doesn't earn his shoe leather, that he is an unpaid servant of the public who is expected to provide advice on all subjects free of charge. Three quarters of our time we were working for nothing, and, like all booksellers, taking a pride in doing so. Then we would get a big order, ship off a tin-lined case full of terrestrial globes to Palestine or India and breathe again.

We realized that we should be ruined if we tried to keep a large stock of new books, but we got together a good collection of new foreign books and a fair stock of old books.

I remember selling a copy of the first edition of Shelley's *Revolt of Islam* to Walter Peck for twenty dollars, and his coming back next day to point out an inscription in Shelley's handwriting. He very nobly offered to let me have it back at the same price, but I am glad to say I was too proud to accept. After that I knew Shelley's handwriting and learnt the value of association copies.

After two years and a half we were still solvent and, taking a friend into partnership, moved to a shop in Gerrard Street.

I had written *Lady into Fox* after the day's work was done and it was published soon after we moved into Gerrard Street.

I was slightly embarrassed at selling my own book, but my shyness wore off after the first half-dozen copies. Then I filled one window with it and vowed to sell a copy to every customer who came in.

"Oh! I don't want *that!* I saw a review and it rather disgusted me. I hate sentimental little books about animals." Such remarks were a moral tonic for me as I stood with my hopes of fame in one hand. But in spite of the natural resistance of my customers I believe that I sold three hundred copies of the first edition of that book personally.

"Thirty-three cents for the shop and fifteen cents in my own pocket," I reflected as I wrapped up each copy and dropped a dollar in the till. It was a great game.

If only there were a few hundred salesmen today who would

take the trouble with my books that I used to take with them myself, I should be buying myself a new Sunbeam instead of a Ford.

One beautiful dark American girl refused my book with unusual vigour—and came back to ask for it next day. That was the origin of the most valued friendship that book brought me, and it brought many friends.

We had let the back room of our shop to Francis Meynell, and after a little while a slender volume—the Book of Ruth—made its appearance. That first publication of the Nonesuch Press, which sold with difficulty at two dollars, is now listed at a hundred. After a time Meynell decided to take the basement below our shop. While he was away on a holiday, the landlord came round with the new lease saying: "If it's not signed today, I shall let it to a film company. "I'll sign it for him," I said. "I'm his partner."

When he returned, I joked with him about having become his partner, but shortly afterward he asked me to be his partner in earnest and I had entered on another branch of the book trade.

When I sold out my share in the bookshop in order to have more time to write, I stayed on in the Nonesuch. Ever since I left the firm, Birrell and Garnett have prospered exceedingly. They have a wonderful stock of second-hand books, but I confess I am happier as a publisher and as an author.

The publisher gets all the pleasures—and most of the profits —and the new bookseller pays in the long run for the publisher's most disastrous mistakes. The new bookseller is the scapegoat of the trade. He stacks up his shop with the rubbish that authors write and publishers foist on him. He is abused, lectured and blamed for everything, and he suffers in silence, bearing the burden of all the books which should never have been written, and if written, then never published.

Thanks to Meynell, the Nonesuch books all sell; no bookseller carries a stock which has decreased in value, so I feel no shame there.

But sometimes when I look at the royalty accounts of my own books, written to please myself alone, I wonder how many are hidden away on the top shelves, mocking the faith that booksellers have had in me. Not a great many, I hope.

The bookseller is the kindest-hearted man alive and extraordinarily long-suffering. He works hard for small returns, he usually spends half his time in giving free advice to everyone in his town, he does all the hard work of the book trade. He sells the books I write and he keeps on selling them. When I think of what that means, I thank my stars that now I only have to write them.

I can hear my sons outside, calling to each other in the garden. When the time comes, shall I hand on the advice my father gave me?

"Never try to write. Never have anything to do with publishing or the book trade."

And I shall add: "Above all, never be a bookseller. That is the worst of all: the hardest work and the worst paid." Yet sometimes I wish I were back in the shop. It was a great game. One was always meeting interesting people, and there was a lot of good talk. But then Birrell was my partner.

X

Early Years in the Book Business

by Adolph Kroch

I do not know of any bookstore amounting to anything that
cannot be traced back to a single dominant personality.

—Lawrence Clark Powell

Adolph Kroch came to the United States from Germany in the
early part of the century and quickly established as a bookseller
in Chicago. The little store in an out-of-the-way location which
he first set up did not stay little and out of the way for long, and
it was not many years before the stores known today as Kroch's
& Brentano's dominated the bookselling scene in the greater
Chicago area. Mr. Kroch retired from active bookselling some
years ago to be succeeded by his son Carl, who has greatly
expanded an already large enterprise. The piece reprinted here,
about his beginnings as a bookseller, is from a paper he read
before a seminar group at the University of Chicago.

I am starting with a terrible confession. I am not what you may
call a regularly trained bookseller. This handicap may encourage those enthusiastic booklovers who would like to select bookselling as a vocation. It may give them words of guidance and
inspiration and some warning. In my home town in Germany,
as a student, I spent most of my time in reading and browsing
around in bookshops. My small allowance, augmented by tutor-
ing, I spent freely on books, gathering together an interesting
private library. Next to reading books and pestering booksellers
with innumerable questions, the reading of book catalogs was
my chief hobby. From my early youth, I felt the amenities of
book collecting, and this incomparable joy taught me the psychology of the book-buyer.

"Such a wonderful profession, that of bookselling," I thought.

All the Kroch's at an ABA convention in Chicago, 1957. From left to right are Adolph Kroch, Mrs. Adolph Kroch, their son Carl Kroch and Mrs. Joan Kroch.

"All you have to do is to read and caress fine books, and even if you have to part with them at times, new ones will replace the loss. You meet charming people who share your book joys, discuss with them your favorite authors, and you add to their happiness by letting them have the books they crave." Little did I know then about the trials and heartaches of bookselling. This is most fortunate, as looking at the bright side of the calling, I failed to see the shadows. This attitude helped me in later years to overcome seemingly insurmountable difficulties. To be surrounded by books was one of my boyish dreams (I still have them), and to those boyish dreams I attribute my business success. I still share with my clients the joys they get from reading the good books which I recommend to them.

My father was a banker, and when he tried to get me to follow his profession, I rebelled. With a bleeding heart, I sold the library I had lovingly assembled and with the proceeds bought a third-class ticket to America. Again, books proved to be my best friends. They made it possible for me to follow instinctively the one vocation I understood; they enabled me to throw off the shackles and prejudices of the Old World and to seek here the fulfillment of my longings. Some native-born Americans do not sufficiently appreciate the thrill and exhilaration of freedom unhampered by class prejudice. The free choice of vocation, the opportunities open alike to everyone willing to work and to struggle, are a sacred heritage we must preserve. When I came here, my first thought was of finding work among books. I heard and read wonders of this "God's country" and was convinced that people with such lofty ideals must be book lovers. I knew my native tongue, I could translate Greek into Latin, I read most of the important English books in translations, but my knowledge of colloquial English was practically nil. After a short odyssey, I found myself as a clerk in a foreign bookstore in Chicago. I was happy, and even the mastery of a book-duster did not dim my enthusiasm. Later, I found that the proper wielding of a duster was the first duty of a bookseller. It helps him to keep his stock neat and clean, to keep his thoughts on books he affectionately dusts and arranges, and to remember titles through intimate association with their physical appearance. I can foretell now the efficiency of a bookselling aspirant from the way he dusts books on the first day of his apprenticeship.

In my first position I learned by contrast, always remembering to treat my prospective book purchasers in the manner I wanted to be treated myself when I was a client. In my first position as a book clerk I began to feel terribly important. Here, I was permitted to talk to strangers, who soon became my friends, about books I loved. I sold them the books without any so-called sales effort, and they came back for more books. And why? Because I offered them something I knew, something I loved, and because I transmitted to them my honest enthusiasm. All this was unobtrusive, genuine and not forced. Unwittingly and subconsciously, I discovered the first three fundamentals of a successful bookseller. They are: (1) to know your books, (2) to become enthusiastic over them, and (3) to transmit this enthusiasm to your clients.

I spent my evenings reading. It was a grand adventure. I was making my own own discoveries. There were Conrad, Hardy, Meredith, Anatole France, Whitman, Strindberg and many other titans of literature who made my life worth living. I was filled with the glamour they instilled in me. My reading was not coordinated, mostly pell-mell, but lusty. I learned the art of rapid reading and read during the evening and late into the night, oftentimes as many as three or four books. I also tried to find out more about my own profession and read books not only on business routine but any books available on bookselling itself. I never could think of bookselling as a cold, matter-of-fact profession. Books to me were "choice legacies of the great, left for the enjoyment of mankind." They must not be traded in as so many pounds of flour but handled with loving care, explained and exhorted but not misrepresented. At the same time I learned that, in spite of our love for books, we must face realities and handle the profession in a business-like manner. The bookseller, without sacrificing his love for good books, must learn to conduct his business in competition with other businesses. A bookstore, well stocked with the best of books, and staffed with intelligent book loving assistants, is of no avail unless it is managed on sound financial principles.

After three years of clerical work, I became restless and dissatisfied. The sphere of my activities became too cramped for my vision, and I felt that the time had come for "love to conquer all." In this case it was my love for books that was to conquer my very limited capital. I resigned my position and began to look around for a store in which I was to prove the soundness of my bookselling principles. I found a small store on a side street with a frontage of twenty feet and a depth of about sixty feet. Simple shelves and tables were installed. For stock I gathered together books that I knew, not merely a haphazard selection, but only such books as appealed personally to my literary taste and with the unfaltering conviction that those books would appeal to my clients. The next task was my window. I realized from the start that the window was to bare my business soul, trying to embrace all good books; and, accordingly, I arranged my first window display. I was so proud of my books that every one was to have a prominent position; the more I loved the book, the more prominent the location. So the window became my real business card, the expression of my individuality. The public noticed the expression, caught the spirit and began to come in. I talked to them about my books; it was I who led the conversation. I spoke to them about the subject I knew best, about the books I loved, and evoked in them the desire to know more about the books. Here is the fourth fundamental principle for the successful bookseller: to make the public want the books you want them to read.

This power to mold the mental requirements of the public must be wielded with tact, discretion and absolute honesty. I succeeded in impressing my clients with the fact that reading good books is not only a pastime, a sport of a thousand thrills, but also a profitable occupation, as it elevates the reader above the dull crowd, offers him the best topic of conversation among intelligent people, and entitles him to the privileges of the only true aristocracy—the aristocracy of mind. He can also share this distinction and pay the finest compliment to his friends' intellects by giving them books as gifts for any and every occasion. To be met in a bookstore known for its good books is really a worth-while distinction.

The mentally alert bookseller has a further opportunity, if not duty, to improve the taste of the reading public. When a genuine effort is made to impress the reader with the beauties of literature in contrast to the shallowness of near-literature, it will usually meet with success. It has to be done gradually, tactfully and persistently. The bookseller's own enthusiasm for literature and his belief that the public is susceptible to good books are his best assistants. Genuine gratitude and affection of attached active buyers will be the bookseller's ample reward.

XI

Censorship
and the Gotham Book Mart

by Frances Steloff

Frances Steloff, one of America's eminent booksellers, founded
The Gotham Book Mart in New York City on January 1, 1920.
Through the years, under Miss Steloff's guidance, the Gotham
became a favored meeting place of many prominent authors,
American and foreign. Though Miss Steloff no longer owns the
shop, having sold it several years ago to a young and enterpris-
ing bookseller, Andreas Brown, she continues an active affilia-
tion as a consultant and lives in tiny quarters above the store.
The reminiscence printed here forms part of Miss Steloff's book,
In Touch with Genius, which is to be published soon.

My first personal encounter with the book censors was in
1931, the result of a catalogue of miscellaneous titles we had
sent out. Apparently a member of the New York Society for the
Suppression of Vice was on our mailing list and received the
catalogue. A number of titles listed were considered by the
Society as obscene. Among these were *Hands Around* by Arthur
Schnitzler, *Mademoiselle de Maupin* by Théophile Gautier, *Songs of
Bilitis* by Pierre Louys, *Jurgen* by James Branch Cabell, *Women in
Love* by D. H. Lawrence, *The Well of Loneliness* by Radclyffe Hall,
The Adventures of Hsi Men Ching and *From a Turkish Harem.* It was
these last two titles that were the basis of the charge against me,
perhaps because they sounded most wicked to the Court. *The
Adventures of Hsi Men Ching* was an abridgement of the famous
Chinese classic by Kin Ping Meh, a book that has been translated
into most of the European languages and that was published in

England under the title *The Golden Lotus,* with an introduction by Arthur Waley of the British Museum. *From a Turkish Harem,* the second book charged by the Court as being obscene, was a collection of Turkish and Persian tales similar to those of Burton's *Arabian Nights.*

The Court of General Sessions finally dismissed the complaint against both books, but the experience had caused me considerable personal anguish, as well as time and expense. It is interesting to recall that the official certificate of dismissal was stamped with a gold seal "bearing a nude figure", as Irving Hoffman pointed out in his column in the *Hollywood Reporter.* This nude figure, I might add, was at least as realistic as any of the drawings in either book.

My next brush with Censorship and John S. Sumner, Secretary of the New York Society for the Suppression of Vice, came in 1935 when I was arrested for selling *If It Die* by André Gide. It was an outrageous incident, for Gide, after all, was one of the world's leading literary men and a member of the French Academy. My plight aroused the concern of many editors of magazines and literary people in general. Christopher Morley gave his entire column, "The Bowling Green," to it in the *Saturday Review of Literature* for January 4, 1936. *The New Republic* and other magazines carried accounts of the trial and acquittal. I received many letters of support from friends and strangers, including many librarians. My friend Sam Putnam wrote as follows: Dear Frances, It was nice seeing you and hearing all about the Gide. I read Morley's article. It is magnificent! I congratulate you on the whole thing and the spunk with which you saw it through. . . .

My last bout with Mr. Sumner occurred in 1945. Charles Henri Ford, editor of *View,* asked if I would have a window for *Arcane 17,* a new book by André Breton and if I would allow Marcel Duchamp and André to arrange the display. It was a huge window and they were at it most of the next day. Part of the display was a beautiful life-size headless figure with a faucet on its thigh, called "Hazy Hardware". The day after the window was done, Mr. Sumner walked in the store, I greeted him and asked what I had done that was wrong. He had a complaint against the window.

"But the model is wearing an apron," I said. Oh, no, it wasn't the model, it was the poster. I went out with him to scrutinize the poster, and he pointed to two small figures, one with her bosom showing.

"Well," I said, "one would have to be terribly evil-minded to see anything wrong with that. Besides, this is an original ·by Matta, and his work hangs in the Museum of Modern Art."

"I can't help that," he replied. "It has to come out."

This time I became bold instead of frightened. I said I would no sooner disturb this window by two fine artists than I would change a painting hanging in the Metropolitan Museum. He gave me his card and told me to let him know by morning what I intended to do about it. I called Charles Ford and he called Duchamp, but before meeting with them I had an idea of my own. I wrote CENSORED on Mr. Sumner's card and stuck it on the spot he objected to. Maya Deren took a photograph of the window which was used in the next issue of *View,* May 1945.

I have always been pretty much of a prude myself and might have cooperated with the censors if they hadn't been so un-believably stupid and without one ounce of discrimination. It makes all the difference in the world if work of this nature is done by an artist or a smut-peddler. Many of our most respected writers and artists have produced works to which censors have objected. D. H. Lawrence had always been one of the best-selling authors in our store, and when *Lady Chatterley's Lover* was first published abroad, he sent us copies from Italy. Somehow they got through customs. When I finished reading it, I couldn't remember any "dirty words" and had to go through it again to find out why it was banned. I used to think that the desire for banned books was a case of forbidden fruits being the sweetest. If all the books were allowed on the shelf with other books, there would be no premium on them, and people who wanted them would soon get their fill. I don't see how healthy-minded people could have their morals corrupted by reading a book, and for those without morals these books might even be some kind of therapy. After all, freedom to read need not mean freedom to disseminate vulgarity and obscenity. We should choose our books as we choose our friends. I wish there were a way to control pornography, but censorship is too high a price to pay.

XII

Bookselling, a Way to International Understanding

by Arnold Toynbee

Professor Toynbee, one of the world's most
distinguished historians, who once was a speaker at
an ABA convention, wrote the following article for
the International Community of Bookseller
Associations.

What is the reader's picture of the bookseller? I mean a serious
reader, the studious reader. I happened to make my own university studies at the University of Oxford, so when I think of
bookshops I naturally always think in terms of the bookshops at
Oxford. Of course, at every great university city you will find
bookshops of that kind and those are the ones with which I am
most familiar. These bookshops are, I am sure, a large and
important part of the student's education. Even at the University
stage, the student is still largely guided by lectures given by
professors, he perhaps receives individual tuition from department heads and so on. But when he enters one of the great
bookshops in his university town, he is learning the extremely
important part of educating himself, because browsing in a
bookshop teaches him to explore the wide world of literature,
and to do this on his own initiative without guidance; he is
learning to find his way for himself and finding his way for
himself is, I think, mostly one of the most important parts of
education.

When human beings browse on books they are educating
their minds. I have very vividly in my mind a picture of people
of all ages and many kinds, standing in the bookshops, taking
books from the shelves, looking at books on the stands, spending perhaps many hours consecutively reading stories and doing
this with books published in all the leading languages of the
world, that is, the leading living languages and in a number of

classical languages as well. I should like to discuss whether the bookseller gains or loses financially by leaving his bookshop entirely open for anyone to come in and browse. I imagine he suffers financially in consequence. Many books are spoiled because several people must read the whole of the book in a bookshop and leave them quite considerably shop-soiled. And some of them are stolen, I am sad to say. And I am sure that must mean an appreciable financial loss on the part of the bookshops. But it also must, I should think, be a financial gain, because some of these browsers become customers and come to stay. I am seventy years old and I still buy a number of books from the bookshop where I used to browse when I was a student. I didn't steal any books, but the bookshops certainly gained by this liberal policy towards browsing.

In any great bookshop you can find all books in all the languages in the world, among the books on sale there. Human beings of all kinds are constantly being prevented by governments from circulating freely all over the world, because of constant government restrictions and regulations hampering this free circulation. And it is surely rather important that the books, which are relatively immune from these restrictions, should continue to circulate freely. And to keep them circulating more or less freely means constant vigilance and constant struggle and constant diplomatic activities on Unesco's part with the governments; constant efforts by the writers, publishers and booksellers organizations. Books are after all the best ambassadors and interpreters. And the booksellers are the couriers of these ambassadors. So long as books can circulate more or less freely all over the world, it does remain possible for the different peoples of the world to increase their understanding of each other. Now that is the objective of first class importance in the human race of our time, because it is necessary to grow into something like a single family. So the international booktrade is one of the best antidotes to isolation and therefore one of the most important safeguards against suicide.

How does one describe the ideal bookshop from the general public's point of view? I should say a bookshop is not merely a place where things are bought and sold, but it is a real seminar for self-education in world understanding. A bookshop should, I am sure, give human browsers of books, opportunities for meeting other people's minds, minds that are disputable to their own minds, not only in space but in time; writers who produced books thousands of years ago, books in other languages on the opposite side of the present-day world.

The ideal bookshop ought to give this browser the opportunity of creating an opinion for himself and to see both sides of a temporary issue. It offers him communistic literature, western democratic literature, atheistic literature and religious literature, Jewish, Hindu and Buddhist literature too. I am convinced that this ought to be our standard of integrity. We ought to give our readers the opportunity of seeing both sides of whatever issue it might be. We ought to have enough confidence in readers to believe that they are human beings capable of comparing and choosing. They will eventually choose the best, though what they think the best may not be what we think best, but they will eventually choose wisely even if they have to go through the process of trial and error. So as far as the booktrade is concerned, the writer is, after all, the primary producer and has a great interest in the sales of the bookseller. In the booktrade I should say there is absolute freedom.

All our literature should be entirely free and the bookseller should serve his fellowmen by making books at all times and in all languages circulate all over the world. I think there is no more valuable public service in the present-day world.

XIII

Lindsay and Crouse Salute the ABA

At the Convention in 1947 Howard Lindsay and Russel Crouse produced merriment aplenty among booksellers and publishers attending with the following stanzas which they sang themselves to the tune of Mr. Gallagher and Mr. Shean. The stanzas are replete with topical allusions which are still familiar today.

Oh, Mr. Lindsay, oh, Mr. Lindsay
No one here has ever heard us sing before
I don't want to throw any doubt on us,
But the audience may walk out on us.
Don't you think we'd better have them lock the door?

Oh, Mr. Crouse, oh, Mr. Crouse,
Any hope of their escape I'll have to douse.
Though the prospects may be black,
If they leave they can't get back.
What's to stop them, Mr. Lindsay?
No unauthorized returns, Mr. Crouse.

Oh, Mr. Lindsay, oh, Mr. Lindsay,
Every bookstore in the country's overstocked.
They are loaded up with war books,
Till they can't take any more books.
And the aisles with juveniles are always blocked.

Oh, Mr. Crouse, oh, Mr. Crouse
It's not that every publisher's a louse,

For these books there is a reason
Though to say it here is treason.
Why do they publish them, Mr. Lindsay?
They don't read them, Mr. Crouse.

Oh, Mr. Lindsay, oh, Mr. Lindsay,
It is sad to hear so many people crab.
They are singing one refrain:
You hear publishers complain
That the book business is very, very drab.

Oh, Mr. Crouse, oh, Mr. Crouse,
No one in the business has a right to grouse.
Of its drabness speak no more,
There is color there galore.
In the bindings, Mr. Lindsay?
Alfred Knopf's shirts, Mr. Crouse.

Oh, Mr. Lindsay, oh, Mr. Lindsay,
There's one publishing house that's very hard to beat.
They sell bookstores each edition,
Then they give them competition
With a bookstore of their own across the street.

Oh, Mr. Crouse, oh, Mr. Crouse,
You haven't told us all about this house.
Still another field they've tilled
With the Literary Guild.
You mean Doubleday, Mr. Lindsay?
I mean Tripleday, Mr. Crouse.

Oh, Mr. Lindsay, oh, Mr. Lindsay,
Literary styles are changing every day.
Once the heroes all were he-men,
Now the he-men turn out she-men
And the women all are rolling in the hay.

Oh, Mr. Crouse, oh, Mr. Crouse,
The ugly head of sex they now arouse.
Once the heroine was a virgin,
Now it's she who does the urgin'.
That's humanity, Mr. Lindsay.
That's the Manatee, Mr. Crouse.

Oh, Mr. Lindsay, oh, Mr. Lindsay,
In this audience are several millionaires,
And all those who are not rich
Surely have the get-rich itch.
Can we tell them how to manage their affairs?

Oh, Mr. Crouse, oh, Mr. Crouse,
To make millions, first you have to start a house,
And then roll in the checks.
In this house you're selling sex.
Disorderly, Mr. Lindsay?
No, publishing, Mr. Crouse.

XIV

A Musical Tribute
to the American Booksellers

words by Michael Flanders
with music by Donald Swann,
sung by them at the ABA Convention, June 1960

Vendor Librorum Floreat

(May the Bookseller Prosper)

It was June in Chicago, and all through the town,
Like everyone else in the States,
They were watching T V. All except for two men
In a bar by the slaughter-house gates
Who were reading a book. I forget what it was:
The Poems of Siegfried Sassoon.
Spinoza, More Peanuts, The Lives of the Saints,
Or *The Case of the Headless Baboon*—
It was one of these five . . . but a book nonetheless,
Which they read by the window that night.
Then a coachload of Booksellers pulled up outside,
Disembarked—and wept tears at the sight
"Oh Flanders and Swann," they remarked, "If 'tis you (and
      'twas)
"How it moves us to see you both here
"Really reading that book—for we're booksellers all—
"Do give us a word of good cheer!"
Then up spake bold Flanders (the one with a beard)
"My word, we'll do better than that."
"Why, good gracious," said Swann, "We'll sing you a song."
Which they did—*At the Drop of a Hat.*

Oh, the bookselling brotherhood's come up to town
They're all on display—and we're marking them down
For a pat on the back; for they take many risks:
What they lose on the books, may they make on the discs.
　　　For a book's to be treasured—a book's to be read—
　　　It's the second best thing to take with you to . . .
Fol-de-rol Folio
Caslon Old Face,
With half-leather binding
And bold lower case!

Good Samaritans all, their stock-taking they'll stop
When a publisher's peddler arrives at their shop.
If he's worn out and weary and nearing his end,
They'll order a gross of *The Beekeeper's Friend.*
　　　So shame on the foes of these dealers in books,
　　　Disputing their sales-sheets and calling them . . .
Fol-de-rol Doubleday, Lippincott Paul,
With Random and Putnam
Macmillan and all!

Then those book-thirsty pirates—the heathen Chinee—
We'll force them to pay us a copyright fee.
Free enterprise—yes, but it's not very nice
To sell standard works at a quarter the price.
　　　Low overhead, undercut, paper-back pest
　　　With a blonde on the jacket exposing her . . .
Fol-de-rol Folio
Caslon Old Face,
With half-leather binding
And bold lower case!

So here is a health to the bold A B A!
They keep selling books—though they swear it don't pay.
Let's all buy a book, then they'll be in the clear.
(If you've got one already—just give them a cheer!)

Hip-hip Hurray!
Hip-hip Hurray!
Hip-hip Hurray!

Here's to best sellers
And choice of the month;
We're all out of stock
"But we'll order at onth."

P. S. That book-loving newspaper sends you these rhymes.
      We must leave a moment to mention *The* . . .
Fol-de-rol fit to print
Prescott and Poore,
All the news and reviews
About lit-er-a-ture!

XV

Christopher Morley
Speaks to the ABA

A man who is impassioned with books has little time or patience
to grow rich by concocting schemes for cozening his fellows.

Christopher Morley in *The Haunted Bookshop*

I seem to remember that the last time the Booksellers' Convention met in Philadelphia—about ten years ago, wasn't it?—a
tenth of a century—was also during a parenthesis of depression.
It is notorious however that the Bad Times Conventions are
always the gayest. This one, I feel, will be no exception. All, even
the publishers, have much on their minds that for a few hours
they are not loth to forget and indulge a pleasing sluice of Lethe.

As a bibliophiladelphian who in these days does not see much
of his first love among cities, I am constrained to say that she is
the ideal convention-ground for an austere and idealizing group
like this. Mrs. Trollope, a hundred years ago, commented on the
fact that the private lives of Philadelphians were peaceful and
demure. They lock their doors at dusk, she said, and spend the
evenings at home reading. Behind the discreet doorways of the
Quaker Oats City there is more spiritual merriment than a
stranger might suppose. Booksellers, always alert to offset the
woes of the trade by the tinsel counterpoise of mirth, will find
it so. Philadelphia, beneath her plain library binding, conceals
many a rubric of gay caprice. Not without reason has she begot-
ten in the past generation the greatest bookseller in the world,
several of the greatest collectors, and the greatest magazine
publishers.

Christopher Morley christens a newly acquired delivery car for Marion Dodd and the Hampshire Book Shop in Northampton, Massachusetts, in 1937.

Collections, the publishers here say, are something terrible; but an era of reddened ink has not been without benefit. There will be less racketeering in the book business for the next five years, and more passion for the realities books were intended to convey. Other fluids besides ink are red and, for the booksellers, aware that some books hold the blood and wine of human life, trade will never be impossible. In our better moments we deal in a merchandise that nothing can destroy. If some of the new books don't seem what they might be, let's sell the older ones. Anyhow, here's luck! We need it.

May 8, 1931 A.D.
(anno depressionis)

XVI

Mark Twain at ABA

Mark Twain was a guest speaker at two ABA Conventions, the first in 1902, the second, six years later. The account which follows is of a meeting held in New York on May 20, 1908 and is reprinted from *Publishers Weekly*.

Mark Twain, upon entering the dining room, received an ovation that lasted fully five minutes. When called upon to address the American Booksellers Association, Mark Twain began by congratulating those present upon their youth, which he considered augured well for his interests, inasmuch as the selling of books should be in the care of young men, enthusiastic and strong enough to cope with the shy and unwilling purchaser. After telling some amusing stories in his inimitable manner, Mark Twain proceeded as follows: "This annual gathering of booksellers from all over America comes together ostensibly to eat and drink, but really to discuss business; therefore I am required to talk shop. I am required to furnish a statement of the indebtedness under which I lie to you gentlemen for your help in enabling me to earn my living. For something over forty years I have acquired my bread by print, beginning with *Innocents Abroad*, followed at intervals of a year or so by *Roughing It*, *Tom Sawyer*, *Gilded Age*, and so on. For thirty-six years my books were sold by subscription. You are not interested in those years, but only in the four which have since followed. The books passed into the hands of my present publishers at the beginning of

1904, and you then became the providers of my diet. I think I may say without flattering you, that you have done exceedingly well by me. Exceedingly well is not too strong a phrase, since the official statistics show that in four years you have sold twice as many volumes of my venerable books as my contract with my publishers bound you and them to sell in five years. To your sorrow you are aware that frequently, much too frequently, when a book gets to be five or ten years old its annual sale shrinks to two or three hundred copies, and after an added ten or twenty years ceases to sell. But you sell thousands of my moss-backed old books every year—the youngest of them being books that range from fifteen to twenty-seven years old, and the oldest reaching back to thirty-five and forty.

"By the terms of my contract my publishers had to account to me for 50,000 volumes per year for five years, and pay me for them whether they sold them or not. It is at this point that you

Mark Twain (left foreground) addresses ABA members at a party given by Harper & Bros. as a feature of the convention in New York in 1902. Seated front left is Mark Twain; next to him is Colonel George Harvey, president of Harper; directly behind Colonel Harvey is Clarence E. Wolcott, ABA president; in the center of the semi-circle is Hamlin Garland, author; to Mr. Garland's left is William Dean Howells, author; Directly behind Mr. Howells is John Kendrick Bangs, author. (Photo courtesy Publishers Weekly*)*

gentlemen come in, for it was your business to unload the 250,000 volumes upon the public in five years if you possibly could. Have you succeeded? Yes, you have—and more. For in four years, with a year still to spare, you have sold the 250,000 volumes, and 240,000 besides.

"Your sales have increased each year. In the first year you sold 90,328; in the second year, 104,851; in the third, 133,975; in the fourth year—which was last year—you sold 160,000. The aggregate for the four years is 500,000 volumes, lacking 11,000.

"Of the oldest book, the *Innocents Abroad*—now forty years old —you sold upwards of 46,000 copies in the four years; of *Roughing It*—now thirty-eight years old, I think—you sold 40,334; of *Tom Sawyer*, 41,000. And so on.

"And there is one thing that is peculiarly gratifying to me: the *Personal Recollections of Joan of Arc* is a serious book; I wrote it for love, and never expected it to sell, but you have pleasantly disappointed me in that matter. In your hands its sale has increased each year. In 1904 you sold 1726 copies; in 1905, 2445; in 1906, 5381; and last year, 6574."

Mark Twain having resumed his seat, Mr. Simon Brentano rose to say that it was rather for the booktrade to thank Mark Twain than for him to thank the booktrade, because in his books the bookseller had an unfailing source of profit and an asset of real value. The whole gathering enthusiastically rose to show their concurrence in Mr. Brentano's sentiments.

There is nothing in the world except a battle like the two weeks before Christmas in a bookshop. There are whole days in which one does not eat anything or have a glass of water or wash one's face. It is like being the mother of ten thousand children and having them all come in at once for cookies and to have their mittens dried.

If you go into any automobile salesroom on Broadway and indicate that you are going to buy a car, the salesman will talk to you for two hours. He can tell you about his car from the bottom screw to the top. But if you ask in a bookshop for Irving's *Sketchbook*, the little girl says sweetly, "Who wrote it, please?" and then she asks somebody else and they ask somebody else, and at last they bring the head of the department from the balcony to ask you if you know who the publisher is.

Our theory was that people are baffled by libraries—when you are confronted by 20,000 books, you will read nothing, but if you have at hand 15 which you feel to be the best current material on any subject important to you, you will read them all. The whole pattern of democracy seems to have become too large.

Madge Jenison in *Sunwise Turn* (1923)

Appendix

I think that I shall never see
A browser who appeals to me—

A man who looks and looks all day
To while the idle hours away;

A man who may in summer sweat
And thereby get an art book wet;

Who likes a wide variety
(Especially pornography);

Whose features are acutely pained
At finding volumes cellophaned.

Book stores are run by fools like me,
But only a browser reads for free.

LEWIS MEYER in *The Customer Is Always*

The Officers of the American Booksellers Association, 1900–1975

ABA Presidents

1900   Henry T. Coates, Porter & Coates, Philadelphia, Pa.

1901   Clarence E. Wolcott, Wolcott & West, Syracuse, N. Y.

1904   W. Millard Palmer, Lyon, Kymer & Palmer Co., Grand Rapids, Mich.

1908   Walter L. Butler, E. S. R. Butler & Son, Wilmington, Del.

1914   Vernor M. Schenck, H. R. Huntting Co., Springfield, Mass. (Mr. Schenck declined the office and was replaced by John J. Wood.)

1915   John J. Wood, Korner & Wood, Cleveland, O.

1916   Ward Macauley, Macauley Bros., Detroit, Mich.

1918   Charles E. Butler, Brentano's, New York.

1920   Eugene L. Herr, L. B. Herr & Son, Lancaster, Pa.

1922   Simon L. Nye, S. Kann Sons Co., Washington, D. C.

1924   Walter V. McKee, Sheehan's Bookstore, Detroit, Mich.

1926   John G. Kidd, Stewart, Kidd, Cincinnati, O.

1928   Arthur Brentano, Jr., Brentano's, New York

1930   George W. Jacobs, Jacobs Book Store, Philadelphia, Pa.

1932   Frank L. Magel, Putnam Book Store, New York

1934   Edmund S. McCawley, E. S. McCawley & Co., Haverford, Pa.

1936   Lewis B. Traver, Traver's Book Store, Trenton, N. J.

1938   August H. Gehrs, Womrath Bookshops & Libraries, New York

1940   Karl Placht, Beacon Book Shop, New York

1942   Nicholas Wreden, Scribner Book Store, New York

1944   Joseph A. Margolies, Brentano's, New York

1946   George A. Hecht, Doubleday Book Shops, New York

1948   Robert B. Campbell, Campbell's Book Store, Los Angeles, Calif.

1950   Allan McMahan, Lehman Book & Stationery Co., Fort Wayne, Ind.

1952 Marion Bacon, Vassar Cooperative Bookshop, Pough-keepsie, N.Y.

1954 Ellsworth R. Young, Phillips Bookstore, Cambridge, Mass.

1956 H. Joseph Houlihan, Morris Book Shop, Lexington, Ky.

1958 Charles B. Anderson, Anderson's Book Shop, Larch-mont, N. Y.

1960 Alva H. Parry, Deseret Book Co., Salt Lake City, Utah

1962 Igor Kropotkin, The Scribner Book Store, New York

1964 Louis Epstein, Pickwick Bookshop, Hollywood, Calif.

1966 Theodore Wilentz, Eighth Street Bookshop, New York

1968 Arnold H. Swenson, Harvard Cooperative Society, Cam-bridge, Mass.

1970 Howard B. Klein, Burrows, Cleveland, O.

1972 Eliot Leonard, Pickwick Book Shop, Hollywood, Calif.

1974 Richard H. Noyes, The Chinook Bookshop, Colo. Springs, Colo.

ABA First Vice-Presidents

1900 Charles W. Burrows, Burrows Brothers, Cleveland, O.

1908 W. H. Cathcart, Burrows Brothers, Cleveland, O.

1913 Vernor M. Schenck, H. R. Huntting Co., Springfield, Mass.

1914 Walter S. Lewis, Strawbridge & Clothier, Philadelphia, Pa.

1918 John G. Kidd, Stewart, Kidd, Cincinnati, O.

1919 Louis A. Keating, Frederick Loeser & Co., Brooklyn, N. Y.

1921 S. D. Siler, Siler's, Inc. New Orleans, La.

1922 J. Joseph Estabrook, Hochschild, Kohn & Co., Bal-timore, Md.

1924 Sidney M. Avery, Brentano's, Washington, D. C.

1925 Hulings G. Brown, Little, Brown & Co., Boston, Mass.

1926 J. Joseph Estabrook, Joseph Horne & Co., Pittsburgh, Pa.

1928 George W. Jacobs, Jacobs Book Store, Philadelphia, Pa.

1929 Paul Elder, Paul Elder & Co., San Francisco, Calif.

1932 John Howell, John Howell, San Francisco, Calif.

1937 Christopher Grauer, Otto Ulbrich Co., Buffalo, N. Y.

1939 Karl Placht, Beacon Book Shop, New York

1940 Alice I. Steinlein, Greenwood Book Shop, Wilmington, Del.

1941 John T. Remington, Remington-Putnam Book Co., Baltimore, Md.

1943 Marion E. Dodd, Hampshire Bookshop, Northampton, Mass.

1946 Otto Grauer, The Otto Ulbrich Co., Buffalo, N. Y.

1948 Joseph A. Margolies, Brentano's, New York

1952 Lewis B. Traver, Traver's Bookstore, Trenton, N. J.

1954 Robert Bangs, Marshall Field & Co., Chicago, Ill.

1956 Sam Pocker, Pocker's, Inc., Washington, D. C.

1958 Alva H. Parry, Deseret Book Co., Salt Lake City, Utah

1960 Arnold H. Swenson, Columbia University Bookstore, New York

1963 Louis Epstein, Pickwick Bookshop, Hollywood, Calif.

1964 Gordon W. Bryant, Charles E. Lauriat Co., Boston, Mass.

1970 Trumbull Huntington, Huntington's Book Stores, Hartford, Conn. (Under the new Constitution and By-Laws adopted by the general membership in 1974 there is to be only one Vice-President. Mr. Huntington was elected to this office.)

ABA Second Vice-Presidents

1900 Edwin B. Curtis, Cunningham, Curtis & Welch, San Francisco, Calif.

1907 Clarence W. Sanders, St. Paul Book & Stationery Co., St. Paul, Minn.

1908 Henry S. Hutchinson, H. S. Hutchinson & Co., New Bedford, Mass.

1911 Edward S. Adams

1912 Vernor M. Schenck, H. R. Huntting Co., Springfield, Mass.

1913 Ward Macauley, Macauley Bros., Detroit, Mich.

1916 Frederic G. Melcher, W. K. Stewart & Co., Indianapolis, Ind.

1918 Henry S. Hutchinson, H. S. Hutchinson & Co., New Bedford, Mass.

1919 John G. Kidd, Stewart, Kidd, Cincinnati, O.

1920 Vernor M. Schenck, H. R. Huntting Co., Springfield, Mass.

1921 Marion E. Dodd, Hampshire Bookshop, Northampton, Mass.

1922 John T. Hotchkiss, J.K. Gill & Co., Portland, Ore.

1923 Walter V. McKee, Sheehan's Bookstore, Detroit, Mich.

1924 W. P. Blessing, Blessing Book Stores, Chicago, Ill.

1925 Stanley G. Remington, Norman-Remington Co., Baltimore, Md.

1926 Edwin I. Hyke, Stix, Baer & Fuller, St. Louis, Mo.

1927 Frank L. Magel, Putnam Book Store, New York

1928 Christopher Grauer, Otto Ulbrich Co., Buffalo, N. Y.

1929 Richard Fuller, Old Corner Book Store, Boston, Mass.

1930 Charles Jackson, Burrows Brothers, Cleveland, O.

1931 W. C. Jacquin, Jacquin & Co., Peoria, Ill.

1932 Will Johnson, W. B. Read & Co., Bloomington, Ill.

1933 J. W. Sutton, Woodbury Book Co., Danville, Ill.

1934 Fred H. Tracht, University of Chicago Bookstore, Chicago, Ill.

1935 E. A. Nichols, President, Illinois Booksellers Ass'n, Champaign, Ill.

1937 Charles M. McLean, Pettibone-McLean, Inc. Dayton, O.

1939 W. W. Goodpasture, Brentano's, Chicago, Ill.

1940 Harry V. Korner, Korner & Wood, Cleveland, Ohio

1943 Lovick Pierce, Cokesbury Book Store, Dallas, Texas

1948 John Barnes, Barnes & Noble, New York

1950 Howard Klein, Burrows Brothers, Cleveland, Ohio

1952 Ellsworth R. Young, Phillips Bookstore, Cambridge, Mass.

1954 Cynthia Walsh, Hampshire Bookshop, Northampton, Mass.

1959 Arnold H. Swenson, Columbia University Bookstore, New York

1960 Louis Epstein, Pickwick Bookshop, Hollywood, Calif.

1963 Doris Thompson, Francis Scott Key Book Shop, Washington, D. C.

1965 Goddard Light, Lighthouse Bookstore, Rye, N. Y.

1968 Howard B. Klein, Burrows, Cleveland, O.

1970 Richard H. Noyes, The Chinook Bookshop, Colo. Springs, Colo.

ABA Third Vice Presidents

1900   Frederic F. Hansell, F. F. Hansell & Bro., New Orleans, La.

1908   J. K. Gill, J. K. Gill Co., Portland, Ore.

1911   Vernor M. Schenck, H. R. Huntting Co., Springfield, Mass.

1912   Ward Macauley, Macauley Bros., Detroit, Mich.

1913   John J. Wood, Korner & Wood, Cleveland, O.

1914   R. F. Fuller, Old Corner Bookstore, Boston, Mass.

1915   Frederic G. Melcher, W. K. Stewart Co., Indianapolis, Ind.

1916   Louis A. Keating, Frederick Loeser & Co., Brooklyn, N. Y.

1918   Charles E. Lauriat, Jr., Charles E. Lauriat Co., Boston, Mass.

1919   Henry S. Hutchinson, H. S. Hutchinson & Co., New Bedford, Mass.

1920   Madge Jenison, Sunwise Turn Bookshop, New York

1921   Whitney Darrow, Charles Scribner's Sons, New York

1922   Adolph A. Kroch, A. Kroch, Inc., Chicago, Ill.

1923   Josephine E. Greene, Brentano's, Chicago, Ill.

1924   Alice M. Dempsey, Gimbel Bros., New York

1925   Anna Morris, J. L. Hudson Co., Detroit, Mich.

1926   Tina J. Cummings, William Hengerer Co., Buffalo, N. Y.

1927   Margaret Ewing, J. K. Gill Co., Portland, Ore.

1928   Veronica Hutchinson, Halle Bros., Cleveland, O.

1929   Bertha Mahoney, The Bookshop for Boys and Girls, Boston, Mass.

1930   Alice Steinlein, Greenwood Bookshop, Wilmington, Del.

1931   Ward Biddle, Indiana University Bookstore, Bloomington, Ind.

1932   Alice Steinlein, Greenwood Bookshop, Wilmington, Del.

1934   C. E. Campbell, Loring, Short & Harmon, Portland, Me.

1935   Lovick Pierce, Cokesbury Book Store, Dallas, Tex.

1937   Helen Stirling, Stanford University Bookstore, Palo Alto, Calif.

1939   Harry Hartman, Harry Hartman—Bookseller, Seattle, Wash.

1940   Ernest Dawson, Dawson's, Los Angeles, Calif.

1943 Robert B. Campbell, Campbell's Bookstore, Los Angeles, Calif.
1948 Allan McMahan, Lehman Book & Stationery Co., Fort Wayne, Ind.
1950 Rose Oller Harbaugh, Marshall Field & Co., Chicago, Ill.
1951 Carol Fleming, Channel Bookshop, New Haven, Conn.
1953 Robert Bangs, Marshall Field & Co., Chicago, Ill.
1954 Alice Carlson, Powers Dry Goods Co., Minneapolis, Minn.
1956 Georgia Leckie, Rich's, Atlanta, Ga.
1959 Louis Epstein, Pickwick Bookshop, Hollywood, Calif.
1960 Igor Kropotkin, The Scribner Bookstore, New York
1962 Nixon Griffis, Brentano's, New York
1963 Trumbull Huntington, Huntington's Book Store, Hartford, Conn.
1964 Alva H. Parry, Deseret Book Co., Salt Lake City, Utah
1965 James F. Albright, Cokesbury Book Store, Dallas, Texas
1967 Stanley P. Hunnewell, The Book Shop, New London, Conn.
1968 Richard H. Noyes, The Chinook Bookshop, Colo. Springs, Colo.
1970 G. Roysce Smith, Yale Co-operative Corp., New Haven, Conn.
1972 Samuel Weller, Weller's Zion Book Store, Salt Lake City, Utah

ABA Secretaries

1900 J. W. Nichols
1904 Harry F. Davis, Pittsburgh, Pa.
1908 Albert B. Fifield, The Edward P. Judd Co., New Haven, Conn.
1911 Walter S. Lewis, Strawbridge & Clothier, Philadelphia, Pa.
1914 Louis A. Keating, Frederick Loeser & Co., Brooklyn, N. Y.
1916 Walter V. McKee, Sheehan's Bookstore, Detroit, Mich.
1918 Frederic G. Melcher, W. K. Stewart Co., Indianapolis, Ind. (Mr. Melcher resigned in the fall of 1920 and was replaced by Belle M. Walker.)

1921   Belle M. Walker, American News Co., New York
1925   Harry V. Korner, Korner & Wood, Cleveland, O.
1928   Ernest Eisele, B. Westerman Co., New York
1929   George W. Jacobs, Jacobs Book Store, Philadelphia, Pa.
1930   Eugene L. Herr, L. B. Herr & Son, Lancaster, Pa.
1932   Alfred B. Carhart, Rodgers Bookstore, Brooklyn, N. Y.
1936   Marion E. Dodd, Hampshire Bookshop, Northampton, Mass.
1939   Marion Bacon, Vassar Cooperative Bookshop, Poughkeepsie, N. Y.
1942   Alice L. Steinlein, Greenwood Book Shop, Wilmington, Del.
1946   Henriette Walter, Post Box Book Shop, New York
1948   Benedict Freud, Gimbel's, Philadelphia
1952   Cynthia Walsh, Hampshire Bookshop, Northampton, Mass.
1954   John Reed, Langley Bookshop, Newton Centre, Mass.
1955   Gordon W. Bryant, Charles E. Lauriat Co., Boston, Mass.
1957   Victoria Wehrum, Bloomingdale's, New York
1962   Gordon W. Bryant, Charles E. Lauriat Co., Boston, Mass.
1964   Elizabeth Young, New Canaan Book Shop, New Canaan, Conn.
1969   Faith Brunson, Rich's, Atlanta, Ga.
1974   Igor Kropotkin, The Scribner Book Store, New York

ABA Treasurers

1901   J. Wilson Hart, New York
1903   August Eckle, New York
1906   Walter L. Butler, E. S. R. Butler & Son, Wilmington, Del.
1908   E. T. Hanford, Hanford & Horton Co., Middletown, N. Y.
1911   Eugene L. Herr, L. B. Herr & Son, Wilmington, Del.
1920   John G. Kidd, Stewart, Kidd, Cincinnati, O.
1926   Stanley G. Remington, The Norman Remington Co., Baltimore, Md.
1932   Ernest Eisele, B. Westerman & Co., New York

1940 Harriet Anderson, The Channel Bookshops, New Haven, Conn. and New York

1941 Nicholas Wreden, The Scribner Book Store, New York

1942 Harold W. Bentley, Columbia University Bookstore, New York

1945 Josephine Kimball, Young Books, New York

1946 Carol Fleming, The Channel Bookshops, New Haven, Conn. and New York

1948 Frederick Wood, Open Book Shop, Bridgeport, Conn.

1950 John Barnes, Barnes & Noble, New York

1951 Charles Reed, Reed's, New Brunswick, N. J.

1953 Gordon W. Bryant, Charles E. Lauriat Co., Boston, Mass.

1956 Charles Reed, Reed's, New Brunswick, N. J.

1957 Arnold H. Swenson, Columbia University Bookstore, New York

1959 John Barnes, Barnes & Noble, New York

1961 H. Joseph Houlihan, Morris Book Shop, Lexington, Ky.

1962 Charles B. Anderson, Anderson's Book Shop, Larchmont, N. Y.

1963 H. Joseph Houlihan, Morris Book Shop, Lexington, Ky.

1964 Trumbull Huntington, Huntington's Book Stores, Hartford, Conn.

1969 Igor Kropotkin, The Scribner Book Store, New York

1974 James Sullivan, Charles E. Lauriat Co., Boston, Mass.

The Board of Trade (*1913–1930*)

The Present Board of Directors (*1930 to date*)

Albright, James F., 1948–1950, 1957–1967

Anderson, Charles B., 1954–1963, 1965–1974 (President 1958–1960)

Arnold, W. H., 1913–1924

Avery, Sidney, 1923–1926

Axelrod, Morris, 1957–1966, 1968–1969

Bacon, Marion, 1935–1941, 1942–1954 (President 1950–1952)

Barnes, John W., 1938–1941, 1946–1948, 1951–1954, 1957–1961

Barnes, William, 1933–1936

Bangs, Robert, 1952–1956

Banker, Robert, 1954–1956

Bates, Elizabeth, 1951–1953

Battle, Gerald N., 1970–

Bentley, Harold, 1940–1943, 1948–1949

Blair, Robert Dike, 1953–1955, 1970–

Brazer, George, 1923–1925

Brentano, Arthur, Jr., 1926–1933, 1942–1946 (President 1928–1930)

Brown, Hulings G., 1920–1923

Browne, D. B., 1921–1927

Brunson, Faith, 1966–1974

Bryant, Gordon W., 1949–1958, 1962–1970

Burkhardt, Charles A., 1917–1920

Butler, C. E., 1913–1920, 1921–1924 (President 1918–1920)

Campbell, Robert B., 1948–1956 (President 1948–1950)

Carhart, Alfred B., 1930–1942

Carlson, Alice, 1952–1956, 1972–1974

Case, Lillian, 1958–1962

Clinger, J. W., 1929–1930

Cobb, Sanford, 1940–1945 (later, President Association of American Publishers)

Cockerill, Angeline, 1958–1962

Crowell, Cedric R., 1923–1938

Davis, William M., 1927–1931

Dodd, Marion E., 1939–1942

Eisele, Ernest, 1925–1928, 1929, 1931–1943

Elder, Paul, 1948–1951

Epstein, Louis, 1956–1968 (President 1964–1966)

Estabrook, Joseph J., 1919–1922, 1924–1930

Fifield, A. B., 1913

Fleming, Carol, 1934–1946, 1948–1953

Fox, Michael Alan, 1973–

Freud, Benedict, 1946–1948, 1951–1952

Friedman, Lillian, 1946–1950

Fuller, R. F., 1917–1923, 1928–1943

Gary, Luther H., 1919–1922

Gately, Bess G., 1953–1955

Gehrs, August H., 1938–1941 (President 1938–1940)

Gordon, Geraldine, 1945–1949

Gould, H. A., 1914–1917

Grauer, C. G., 1922–1925

Grauer, Otto, 1941–1948

Grant, J. M., 1913

Greaney, Viola, 1955–1961

Greene, Holley III, 1969–1970

Griffis, Nixon, 1954–1963

Gross, Sidney, 1970–1972

Hackett, E. Byrne, 1914–1920

Hale, Robert D., 1971–

Harbaugh, Rose Oller, 1944–1950

Hartog, Alfred, 1927–1930

Hecht, George A., 1941–1954 (President 1946–1948)

Hedman, Eleanor, 1973–

Herr, Eugene L., 1913–1917 (President 1920–1922)

Hirsch, Peter, 1974–

Hoag, Robert, 1945–1948

Holliday, Terence, 1936–1939

Hotchkiss, John T., 1922–1925

Houlihan, H. Joseph, 1953–1962, 1963–1972, 1974– (President 1956–1958)

Hunnewell, Stanley P., 1960–1968

Huntington, Trumbull, 1960–1969, 1970–

Hutchinson, H. S., 1913–1920

Jackson, Charles K. 1941–1944, 1946–1951

Jacobs, George W. 1921–1938 (President 1930–1932)

Kain, Margaret, 1962–1968

Keating, Louis A., 1918–1924, 1930–1933

Kidd, John G., 1926–1934 (President 1926–1928)

Kimball, Josephine, 1937–1946

Klein, Howard B., 1949–1950, 1964–

1972 (President 1970–1972)
Korner, H. V., 1919–1921
Kroch, Adolph A., 1928–1944
Kroch, Carl A., 1951–1960, 1965–
Kropotkin, Igor, 1955–1966, 1967–
(President 1962–1964)
Kuhl, Nevin, 1965–1972

Lacey, F. D. 1917–1927
Lauriat, Charles E., Jr., 1917–1920
Leckie, Georgia, 1951–1959
Leonard, Eliot, 1959–1965, 1968–
1974 (President 1972–1974)
Levin, Morton L., 1962–1965
Levinson, Harry A., 1937–1947
Lewis, W. S., 1913–1929
Lichtenstein, Elsa, 1969–
Light, Goddard, 1959–1968, 1970–
1975
Loos, John, 1919–1922
Lorentz, Adrien (Bud), 1973–
Lowery, Elizabeth M., 1956–1965

Macauley, Ward, 1913–1921 (President 1916–1918)
Magel, Frank L., 1924–1942 (President 1932–1934)
Mahony, Bertha, 1920–1923
Margolies, Joseph A., 1944–1948 (President 1944–1946)
Martin, Roberta, 1941–1947
McCawley, Edmund S., 1933–1939 (President 1934–1936)
McGee, Robert, 1970–
McFarland, L. W., 1922–1928
McGreevy, JoAnn, 1974–
McKee, Walter V., 1918–1921, 1924–1929 (President 1924–1926)
McLean, Charles, 1931–1934
McMahan, Allan, 1947–1948, 1950–1955, 1957–1966 (President 1950–1952)
McNulty, Gerald, 1972–
Melcher, Frederic G., 1917–1920 (later, President R.R.Bowker Co.)
Morehouse, Edward, 1917–1921

Noyes, Richard H., 1965– (President 1974–)
Nye, Simon L., 1918–1931 (President 1922–1924)

Parker, Helen, 1943–1945
Parry, Alva H., 1956–1965 (President 1960–1962)
Pettibone, Walter, 1944–1947
Pierrepont, John, 1954–1955
Pitman, Allan, 1928–1932
Placht, Karl, 1934–1945 (President 1940–1942)
Pocker, Samuel M., 1950–1953, 1955–1958
Potter, Fred H., 1961–1968

Reed, Charles, 1948–1953, 1955–1957
Reed, John, 1951–1954
Remington, John T., 1940–1942, 1943–1946
Remington, Stanley G., 1923–1937

Sallade, George Wahr, 1953–1956
Saltmarsh, Robert C., 1936–1937
Schenck, Vernor M., 1913–1918 (President-elect 1914)
Schulte, T. E., 1917–1919, 1925–1940
Schwartz, Harry W., 1952–1955, 1966–1969
Schwartz, Leonard, 1965–1968, 1972–1974
Seaman, Walter L., 1950–1952
Seiler, A. G., 1917–1919, 1927–1935
Seligman, Sylvia, 1974–
Sims, Luise, 1947–1951
Smith, G. Roysce, 1968–1971 (Executive Director 1972–)
Steinlein, Alice L., 1938–1942
Stockell, Alice, 1945–1948
Strouse, Elizabeth, 1967–1968
Sullivan, James, 1972–1975
Swenson, Arnold H., 1954–1963, 1964–1973, 1974– (President 1968–1970)

Thompson, Doris, 1956–1965, 1966–1969

Traver, Lewis B., 1930–1952 (President 1936–1938)

Udin, Anne, 1956–1965

Walsh, Cynthia, 1950–1959

Wehrum, Victoria, 1955–1964, 1965–1968

Welch, Mary, 1950–1951

Weller, Samuel, 1968–1974

Welsh, Pat M., 1972

Wilentz, Theodore, 1962–1968 (President 1966–1968)

Wilson, Carl K., 1948–1950

Wilson, Ralph, 1922–1931

Wood, Frederick, 1942–1948

Wood, John J., 1914–1916 (President 1914–1916)

Wreden, Nicholas, 1941–1944 (President 1942–1944)

Young, Elizabeth, 1963–1971

Young, Ellsworth R., 1948–1956 (President 1954–1956)

Honorary Life Members of ABA

Honorary life memberships in ABA are awarded, on their retirement from active bookselling, to those booksellers who have made signal contributions both to the profession and to the Association. The date in parentheses indicates the year of their retirement.

James F. Albright (1968), formerly with Cokesbury Book Store of Dallas and a former director of ABA.

Harriet Anderson (1956), a former co-owner of the Channel Book Shop in New York and later New Haven and a former director of ABA.

Marion Bacon (1966), former head of the Vassar Cooperative Bookshop and a past president of ABA.

Gordon Bryant (1972), formerly president of Lauriat's in Boston and for many years a director of ABA.

Lillian Case (1964), formerly book buyer at St. Paul Book & Stationery and a former director of ABA.

Angeline Cockerill (1966), formerly head of the book department at H. & S. Pogue in Cincinnati and a former director of ABA.

Louis Epstein (1972), founder and former owner of Pickwick Bookshop in Hollywood, California, and a past president of ABA.

J. Joseph Estabrook (1958), formerly with Hochschild, Kohn & Co. of Baltimore and Joseph Horne & Co. of Pittsburgh and a past officer of ABA.

W. W. Goodpasture (1970), formerly with Kroch's & Brentano's, Chicago, and a former officer of ABA.

Geraldine Gordon (1951)

Rose Oller Harbaugh (1952), formerly book buyer for Marshall Field in Chicago and a former ABA director.

Charles Jackson (1951), formerly with Burrows Brothers in Cleveland and a former director of ABA.

Adolph Kroch (1951), founder of Kroch's Bookstore in Chicago and a former officer of ABA.

Allan McMahan (1971), former owner of Lehman Book &

Staionery in Fort Wayne, Indiana and a past president of
ABA.

Joseph A. Margolies (1960), formerly with Brentano's in New
York and a past president of ABA.

Alva H. Parry (1973), formerly head of the Deseret Book Company in Salt Lake City and a former president of ABA.

Karl Placht (1963), former owner of Beacon Book Shop in New
York and a past president of ABA.

Walter L. Seaman (1965), formerly with the Methodist Publishing House in Nashville and a former director of ABA.

Lewis B. Traver (1967), former owner of Traver's Book Store
in Trenton, New Jersey and a past president of ABA.

Anne Udin (1970) formerly book buyer for the Higbee Company in Cleveland and a former director of ABA.

Elizabeth Young (1973), formerly co-owner of the New Canaan
Book Shop in New Canaan, Connecticut and a former
officer of ABA.

ABA Executive Directors

(Before 1956 this officer was called the executive secretary)

1925   Ellis W. Meyers
1933   Robert M. Coles
1943   Harriet S. Coles (Acting)
1946   Gilbert E. Goodkind
1952   (February to June)   Dorothy McKenzie (Acting)
1952   (June to March 1953)   Robert Pilpel
1953   (March to June)   Dorothy McKenzie (Acting)
1953   (June—) Joseph A. Duffy
1972   G. Roysce Smith

Irita Van Doren Book Award

1967   William I. Nichols
1968   Miss Mildred Smith

1969 Robert Cromie
1970 Edward A. Weeks
1971 Cass Canfield
1972 Norman Cousins
1973 Theodore Solotaroff
1974 Kenneth D. McCormick

Winners of John Barnes "Publisher of the Year" Awards

1964 Harper & Row
1965 Doubleday & Company and Crown Publishers
1966 Harper & Row and Antheneum Publishers
1967 Doubleday & Company and Crown Publishers
1968 McGraw-Hill Book Company and Farrar, Straus and Giroux
1969 J.B. Lippincott Company and Abingdon Press
1970 Harper & Row and Charles E. Tuttle Co., Inc.